Earrings

VISUAL™
PROJECT GUIDE

Earrings

VISUAL™
PROJECT GUIDE

Step-by-step instructions for 30 gorgeous designs

Chris Franchetti Michaels

WILEY

John Wiley & Sons, Inc.

Credits

Acquisitions Editor
Pam Mourouzis

Senior Project Editor
Donna Wright

Copy Editor
Emily Hinkel

Technical Editor
Marti Icenogle

Editorial Manager
Christina Stambaugh

Vice President and Publisher
Cindy Kitchel

Vice President and Executive Publisher
Kathy Nebenhaus

Interior Design
Kathie Rickard
Elizabeth Brooks

Photography
Chris Franchetti Michaels
Matt Bowen

Earrings VISUAL Project Guide

For general information on our other products and services or to obtain technical support please contact our Customer Care Department within the U.S. at (877) 762-2974, outside the U.S. at (317) 572-3993, or fax (317) 572-4002.

John Wiley & Sons, Inc., also publishes its books in a variety of electronic formats and by print-on-demand. Not all content that is available in standard print versions of this book may appear or be packaged in all book formats. If you have purchased a version of this book that did not include media that is referenced by or accompanies a standard print version, you may request this media by visiting http://booksupport.wiley.com.

For more information about Wiley products, visit us at www.wiley.com.

Library of Congress Control Number: 2012948551
ISBN: 978-1-118-08344-4 (pbk)
ISBN: 978-1-118-23665-9; 978-1-118-26159-0; 978-1-118-22275-1 (ebk)

Printed in the United States of America

10 9 8 7 6 5 4 3 2 1

Book production by John Wiley & Sons, Inc., Composition Services

Updates to this book and the design templates are available on the Downloads tab at this site: www.wiley.com/go/earringsvisualprojectguide.

About the Author

Chris Franchetti Michaels is a writer and jewelry artisan specializing in beaded designs, wirework, and metal fabrication. She is the author of several popular craft books, including *Teach Yourself VISUALLY Jewelry Making & Beading, More Teach Yourself VISUALLY Jewelry Making,* and *Teach Yourself VISUALLY Beadwork*. Chris has appeared on several episodes of the DIY Network television show *Jewelry Making* and is the Guide to Beadwork on About.com. Visit her Website www.beadjewelry.net for more help and inspiration.

Acknowledgments

To everyone who worked on this book, I owe a big thank you. Special thanks to Pam Mourouzis and Donna Wright, who managed to keep everything on track and organized. Emily Hinkel's and Marti Icenogle's fresh eyes were truly invaluable. Matt Bowen not only photographed the earrings and tools in this book, but photo edited my own attempts at the project steps. As always, thanks to my agent, Marilyn Allen, for her continued encouragement, and to Dennis for his patience and support.

Table of Contents

Table of Contents

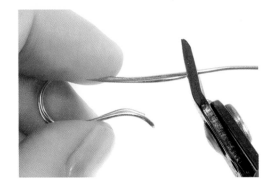

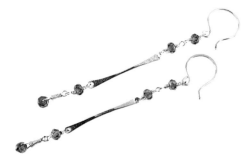

Table of Contents

CHAPTER 9   Sparkle and Glam   208

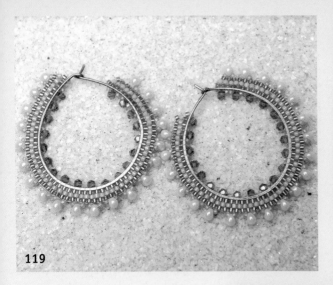

119

167

58

183

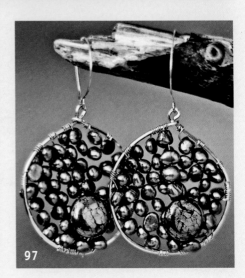

97

60

64

49

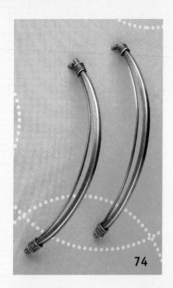

74

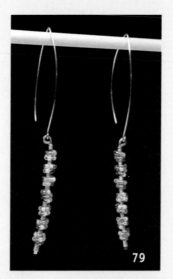

79

110

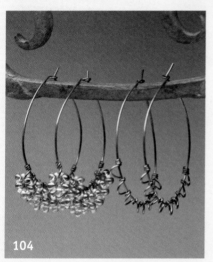

104

128

135

42

83

46

213

92

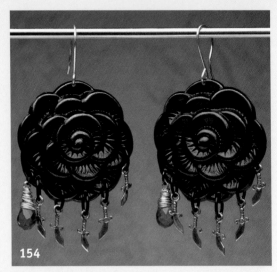

154

140

180

131

70

145

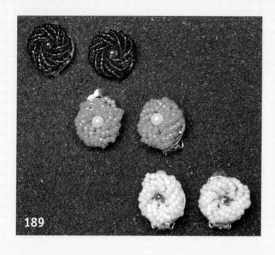

189

229

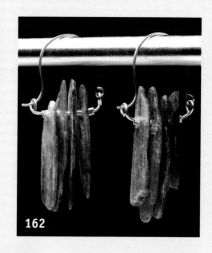

162

195

199

210

157

222

218

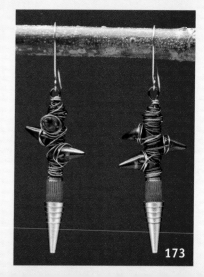

173

CHAPTER 1

Getting Started

In this introductory chapter, you'll learn the benefits of crafting your own earrings, what to think about when creating custom designs, and which tools and supplies you need to complete the projects in this book.

Design Considerations for Earrings

Handmade earring designs can be customized in limitless ways. While reading this book, you may think of interesting ways to vary the projects, and you may even be inspired to develop your own designs from scratch. Here are some tips for successful custom earring design.

EARRING WEIGHT

The weight of the components you use to make an earring is important for two reasons:

- Heavy earrings can cause discomfort by pulling your earlobes, and may even stretch them over time.

- Depending on an earring's shape, its weight contributes to how well it stays positioned on your ear. This is especially true for post and clip-on earrings, where extra weight can cause earrings to tip forward when you wear them.

EARRING SAFETY

Avoid shapes or configurations that may be prone to snagging on clothing or other items. Also take care to file wire ends to prevent them from scratching skin, especially with wires that pass through pierced ears. Learn how to file wire ends properly in the section "File Wire" in Chapter 2.

METAL TYPES

Some metals are prone to causing skin sensitivity. This is an important consideration for ear wires because they come into such close contact with skin—particularly if you have skin allergies or make earrings for someone who may. Learn more in the section "Select Wire for Earrings" in Chapter 2.

A variety of earring types

Reasons to Make Your Own Earrings

If you love earrings, that may be reason enough to start making them. But there are also practical reasons to become your own earring designer.

COORDINATE DESIGNS WITH YOUR WARDROBE

When you shop for earrings, it can be difficult to find the perfect styles, sizes, and colors to coordinate with your unique wardrobe. Once you have the skills to make your own earrings, you can select colors and textures that enhance your ensembles and best communicate your style.

SELECT YOUR OWN METALS

Many affordable, store-bought earrings have ear wires made from mystery metals. You know that they are silver colored, gold colored, or antiqued, but you may not know whether they contain nickel (a common skin irritant) or lead (which is potentially toxic), or whether they have thin platings that are bound to wear off over time. When you make earrings, you can select metals that meet your needs and standards.

EXPERIMENT WITH NEW TECHNIQUES

Earring projects are great for experimenting with new jewelry making techniques without making big commitments. The techniques you learn are transferrable to an endless variety of larger-scale projects, such as bracelets and necklaces. The projects in this book cover a range of techniques, from wire wrapping to bead weaving and even bead embroidery. In making them, you just might discover a new path that you'd never thought of taking before.

TIP

Earrings can be inspirations for pendants

As you work through the projects in this book, think about how you might alter the designs to make matching pendants for necklaces. To learn more about making necklaces, see the books *Teach Yourself VISUALLY Jewelry Making & Beading* and *More Teach Yourself VISUALLY Jewelry Making*. To enhance your beadwork skills, see the book *Teach Yourself VISUALLY Beadwork: Learning Off-Loom Beading Techniques One Stitch at a Time*.

Project Tools and Materials

This section provides a general overview of the jewelry making supplies used throughout this book. The tools and materials required to make the individual earrings are listed at the beginning of each project. You can find most supplies at general jewelry making stores and websites, such as www.firemountaingems.com and www.rings-things.com. For harder-to-find items, suggested online resources are included in the project supply lists.

Wirework Supplies

Wire is available in many metal types, sizes, and shapes. Learn more about it in the section "Select Wire for Earrings" in Chapter 2.

Jewelry making pliers are the most important tools for making earrings. The projects in this book use *flat nylon jaw pliers* (a), *round nose pliers* (b), *chain nose pliers* (c) (sometimes two pairs), *flat nose pliers* (d), *bail-making pliers* (e), and *bracelet-bending pliers* (f). Be aware that chain nose pliers are available in a straight style (like those shown) and also a curved, or *bent nose*, style, which is used in some of the projects in this book.

Side cutters (g) are wire cutters that create a flush (or near flush) cut on wire on one side of the pliers and a jagged cut on the other. Purchase a smaller pair for intricate cuts and a heavier pair for cutting thick wire.

Needle files are small metal files used by jewelers. They are available in a variety of shapes and degrees of coarseness (called *cuts*). The projects in this book use a standard, medium-cut, flat needle file (h).

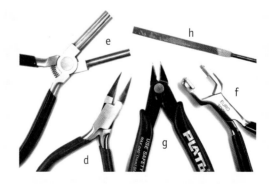

Mandrels are objects that you can wrap wire around to create a particular wire shape. You can buy ready-made mandrels in a variety of shapes and sizes or use common household objects, such as pill bottles, markers, and wooden dowels.

Chasing hammers (a) and *rawhide hammers* (b) are used to flatten, stiffen, or texturize wire that you place on the surface of a *steel bench block* (c).

The chemical *liver of sulfur* is used to darken, or create a *patina* on, metals that contain copper. You use it with latex or nitrile gloves and paper towels. The liquid liver of sulfur used in this book was purchased at www.dickblick.com.

Fine steel wool and *steel bristle brushes* are used to back off a patina or create a brushed finish on metal. You can find these materials at hardware stores as well as at jewelry supply stores.

Beading Supplies

Beads are available in an endless variety of materials, shapes, and sizes. Regular beads, such as *round beads* (a), have holes that run through their centers. *Briolettes* (b) come to a point at one end. Some suppliers refer to briolettes as *teardrop beads.*

Other styles of beads used in the projects in this book include *magatamas* (c), *drop beads* (d), *Twin beads* (e), *Tila beads* (f), *cylinder beads* (g), and *round seed beads* (h).

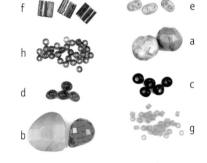

Beading needles (i) look like sewing needles but have eyes small enough to fit through bead holes.

The two most common types of beading thread are *nylon thread* (j) and *bonded polypropylene thread* (k). *Thread conditioner* (l) is used to coat thread to remove static and help reduce knotting.

Beading scissors (or *embroidery scissors*) (m) are used to cut nylon thread. A *thread burner* (n) is a tool that cuts nylon and polypropylene thread by melting it. You can also use *children's craft scissors* (o), a *hobby knife* (p), or side cutters (see page 7) to cut polypropylene thread.

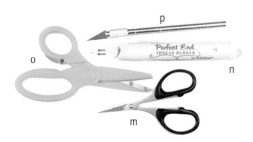

9

Beading mats are pieces of fabric that help keep your round beads from rolling away.

Bead dishes are small ceramic dishes that make it easy to pick up tiny beads with your beading needle.

When you work with very small beads, you may find it helpful to use a *magnifier*. You can purchase one that you wear as a headband, as shown, or use a tabletop version.

A *bead reamer* is a pointed, rough metal bit that you can use to smooth or enlarge the holes in some beads.

Bead backing (a) is an interfacing style of fabric used for bead embroidery.

Because its edges do not unravel, *ultrasuede* (b) is the preferred material for covering the back sides of bead embroidery pieces.

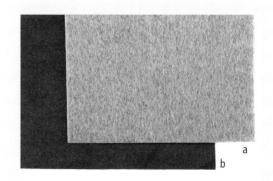

a

b

Ready-Made Findings and Components

Some projects in this book use ready-made, rather than handmade, *ear wires* (a) and *earring posts* (b). You can save time, or achieve a particular look, by purchasing them in a variety of styles, sizes, and metals.

Earring post backs (also called *clutches* or *earring nuts*) (c) slide onto earring posts to keep them from falling off of your ears. They are also available in a variety of styles.

Clip-ons (d) are earring findings for non-pierced ears, or for when you want to create a certain vintage look. The clip-ons used in this book have pronged pads for attaching *perforated discs* (sometimes called *mesh screens*) (e).

Jump rings (f) are circles or ovals of wire used to connect components.

Head pins (g) are short lengths of wire with nail heads, metal balls, or other decorations at one end to prevent beads from falling off.

Filigree (h) is a flat or rounded decorative metal sheet inspired by handmade filigree metalwork.

Fold-over cord ends (i) are used for connecting cord and other components, such as feathers, to earring findings.

Rhinestone chatons (j) are loose rhinestones with pointed backs.

Cabochons (k) have flat bottoms for gluing or setting. They can be made of glass, plastic, gemstone, or natural materials, such as shell.

Jewelry chain (l) is available in a broad range of metals, finishes, shapes, and sizes. You can purchase it unfinished (without clasps) and connect it to other components. You can use ready-made *chain ends* (m) to finish *rhinestone chain* (n).

General Craft Supplies

Hole punching pliers (a) are designed to pierce holes in thin metal sheet. You can also use them to pierce other soft materials, such as plastic. They are available in a range of sizes; the 1.25mm round size is used in this book.

Permanent markers (b) are useful for drawing patterns onto bead backing for bead embroidery.

Keep a pair of *regular scissors* (c) on hand for cutting out paper patterns, extra-sharp *fabric scissors* (d) for cutting bead backing and ultrasuede, and *utility shears* (e) for cutting stronger materials, such as plastic.

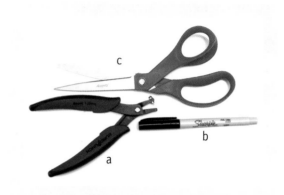

You can use *acrylic craft paint* (f) to color all kinds of jewelry components. In this book, they are used to color plastic (Lucite) cabochons.

Artist pigment (g) is a concentrated colored powder.

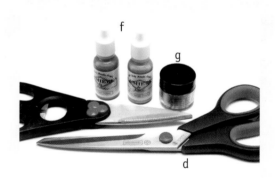

Disposable *sponge-tip applicators* (h) are used to apply paint and ink to jewelry components.

Instant bond glue (i), such as Krazy Glue, works well for securing tiny knots in beading thread.

E6000 (j) is an industrial-strength clear glue used to bond jewelry components.

Toothpicks (k) are useful for applying small amounts of glue, painting small areas, and—when used with *bees-wax* (l)—picking up and placing rhinestone chatons.

You can use *clear acrylic spray* to seal jewelry components after painting them.

Keep a ruler and a *sliding brass gauge* on hand for measuring wire, beads, chain, bead backing, and other materials.

A *prong pusher* is a common jeweler's tool used for bending down prongs on jewelry components.

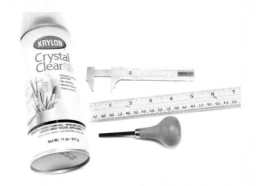

A hobby knife (see page 9) comes in handy for cutting polypropylene thread, chipping off chunks of beeswax to help place chatons, and making small holes in ultrasuede.

Apoxie Sculpt is a brand of two-part epoxy clay that you can use to set chatons or mold into various shapes. It cures to become solid plastic.

Leather cord is a versatile jewelry making component that is easy to cut to any length.

Cardboard makes a good disposable work surface for glue, spray sealer, or epoxy clay.

Always keep a set of standard craft safety supplies on hand. Wear a *dust mask* whenever you work with fine particles (such as artist pigment) and *ear plugs* during noisy tasks (such as hammering). Also wear *safety glasses* whenever you hammer or trim wire or when you cut chain.

CHAPTER 2

Essential Techniques

This chapter reviews the basic jewelry making techniques used throughout this book. Look for references to this chapter at the beginning of each project.

Basic Wirework

Wirework skills are essential to most earring projects. You can use wire to make ear wires, form hoops, create connectors and drops, and wrap beads and other components. To learn even more wirework techniques, see the book *Wire Jewelry VISUAL Quick Tips*.

Select Wire for Earrings

When deciding which wire to use, consider the wire's gauge, metal type, shape, and temper. Although each project in this book recommends which wire to use for best results, you can refer to this section for help selecting wire for your own designs or for making substitutions.

WIRE GAUGE

Gauge refers to the thickness of wire. The smaller the gauge, the thicker the wire. The chart on the following page provides the approximate diameters of the most popular American wire gauges ("AWG") used in earring projects, along with their suggested uses.

METAL TYPE

The best metals for handmade earrings are *nonferrous* (non-iron-containing) metals that are unlikely to irritate sensitive skin. Skin irritation from earrings is usually caused by metals that contain nickel. Gold, fine silver, sterling silver (including Argentium silver), brass, bronze, and copper are normally nickel free. However, some people experience skin reactions from copper and copper-containing alloys, such as sterling silver. Copper can also create green or black markings on skin.

TIP

A simple rule for selecting ear wire gauge

Most ear wires are made from 22- or 20-gauge wire. Use 22-gauge wire to give ear wires a more delicate look or to make designs that involve lots of wrapping. Use 20-gauge wire for a more substantial look or to create sturdier findings that are less likely to lose their shape.

Wire Gauge	Actual Size	Diameter in Millimeters	Diameter in Inches	Use for
16		1.29	.051	Larger jump rings, heavy bead links for beads with large holes
18		1.02	.040	Jump rings, head and eye pins, simple bead links, heavier ear wires
19		.912	.036	Same uses as 18 gauge
20		.812	.032	Smaller jump rings, head and eye pins, smaller simple bead links, heavier wrapped bead links, ear wires
21		.723	.028	Head and eye pins, heavier wrapped bead links, ear wires
22		.644	.025	Head and eye pins, wrapped bead links, ear wires
24		.511	.020	Standard wrapped bead links
26		.405	.016	Small or fine wrapped bead links

WIRE SHAPE

Although the most common wire shape is round (a), jewelry wire is also available in half-round (b), low-dome (c), square (d), triangle (e), and flat (f) shapes. Round wire is best for wrapping around beads and other components, while shaped wire is good for creating structural elements and adding decorative interest.

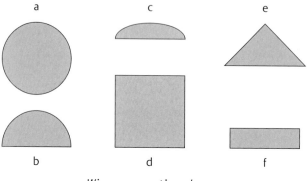

Wire cross-section shapes

TEMPER

Temper describes a wire's degree of stiffness. *Hard temper* wire is much stiffer than *soft temper* wire. To make earring findings, you need wire that is soft enough to bend but stiff enough that it holds its shape.

The projects in this book use *dead-soft* and *half-hard* temper wire. Dead-soft wire is easier to bend and wrap. Half-hard wire is more difficult to bend but holds its shape better than dead-soft wire.

FAQ

Can I change the temper of wire?

Yes. You can increase wire's temper slightly by running it through nylon jaw pliers (see the next section, "Straighten, Cut, and File Wire"), hammering it, or simply bending it back and forth. This process is called *work-hardening*. Keep in mind that if you work-harden your wire too much, it will eventually become brittle and may break.

You can make wire softer by heating it with a butane torch. This process is called *annealing*. The projects in this book do not use annealing, but you can learn more about it in advanced metal fabrication books or by taking a class.

Straighten, Cut, and File Wire

STRAIGHTEN WIRE

When you unroll new wire from its coil or spool, the wire is usually curved and may be a little bent. You can straighten it out by running it through the closed jaws of nylon jaw pliers.

Hold one end of the wire securely with your fingers or chain nose pliers. Or, if the wire is still on the spool, as shown, you can simply hold the spool. Grasp the wire with nylon jaw pliers close to the end you're holding, and pull them firmly along the entire length of the wire. Repeat this process until the wire is straight enough to work with; it rarely needs to be perfectly straight.

Keep in mind that straightening wire increases its temper. This is beneficial when you want to make wire stiffer for components like ear wires. However, it also makes wire slightly more brittle and more difficult to bend.

TIP

You can also straighten wire mid-project

With projects that involve lots of wrapping, you may find that your wire becomes bent or slightly kinked before you finish a task. In that case, hold onto the component you are working on in one hand, and use your other hand to straighten the wire with nylon jaw pliers. Only do so as necessary to avoid work-hardening your wire too much and making it prone to breaking.

CUT WIRE

You can make the wire ends on wire jewelry components flat (a) rather than jagged (b) by making *flush-cuts*. Side cutters (see "Wirework Supplies" in Chapter 1) create flush-cuts with the flat sides of their jaws. When instructions call for a flush-cut, be sure to position your cutters accordingly.

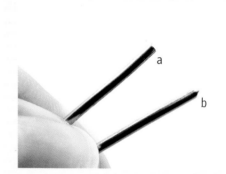

If you flush-cut a length of wire from a coil or spool, remember that the end of the remaining wire is now jagged. You can make it flush by snipping off its end with the flat side of your cutters.

Whenever you trim wire, be sure to aim the tapered sides of the blades away from you; the wire shoots out from that side and can pose a safety hazard. It's also a good idea to wear safety glasses when you cut wire.

FILE WIRE

You can file wire using standard-size jeweler's metal files or needle files (see "Wirework Supplies" in Chapter 1).

FLAT-FILING

When you *flat-file* the end of wire, you use the file to perfect and smooth out its flush-cut. Hold the end of the wire firmly between your fingers, and run the file along the end with the file perpendicular to the wire. Keep in mind that most files work in only one direction: filing away from you. You can extend the life of your file by lifting it off of the metal between strokes.

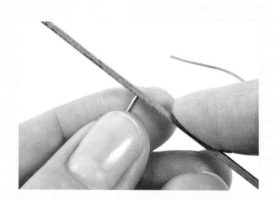

DEBURRING

Deburring is the process of rounding the end of cut wire and removing any sharp or jagged edges. It is important to debur the ends of ear wires so that they do not scratch your ears when you put them on.

To debur wire, hold it the same way you would for flat filing. Gently run the file over the edges of the wire end at a 45-degree angle, all the way around the circumference of the wire.

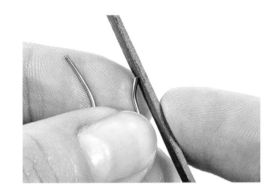

Round the wire end by running the file up, over, and down the wire several times (a). Use your finger to check for any remaining sharp areas, and continue filing as necessary until the wire end feels completely smooth (b).

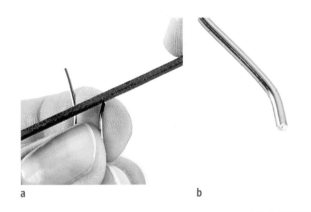

a   b

Can I use a file to remove scratches on wire?

Wire can get scratched by your pliers as you work. Small imperfections are often best left alone. They tend not to distract from the beauty of hand-made jewelry. For larger scratches, you can use a file to minimize their appearance. Just take care not to compromise the wire's strength by removing too much metal, and never file scratches on plated or colored wire, because filing removes their finishes. To learn how to avoid scratches from tools, see the FAQ "How can I avoid marring wire with my pliers?" later in this chapter.

FAQ

Bend, Shape, and Hammer Wire

To review the types of pliers and other tools mentioned in this section, see the section "Project Tools and Materials" in Chapter 1.

BEND WIRE

Make curves near the end of wire by grasping the wire with round nose or bail-making pliers (shown) and rotating the pliers toward you or away from you (a).

Make curves midway along a piece of wire by using your fingers to bend the wire down on either or both sides of the pliers (b).

Make angled bends in wire by grasping it with flat nose (shown) or chain nose pliers and rotating the pliers toward you (c).

Make tight U-shaped bends by first making an angled bend, and then using your fingers to bend down the other side of the wire (d).

Make a loop at the end of wire by grasping it with round nose pliers and rotating the pliers in a rolling motion away from you (e). You may need to reposition the pliers and roll again to complete a full loop.

Make a loop midway along a piece of wire by grasping it with round nose pliers and using your fingers to bend the wire up over the pliers on both sides until the wire crosses (f).

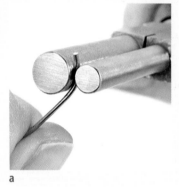

a

b

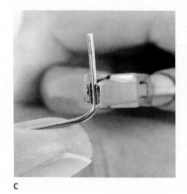

c

d

e

f

SHAPE WIRE

You can use mandrels to bend wire into specific shapes. To make a shape, use your fingers to press the wire firmly all the way around the mandrel, allowing the ends of the wire to overlap on the other side. When you remove the wire from the mandrel, the wire will spring back a little and create a slightly larger shape than the mandrel itself. This effect is more pronounced with half-hard wire than it is with dead-soft wire.

You can also use mandrels to adjust or correct the shapes of large hoops or frames of wire, such as those closed at their tops by wrapping (see the section "Wrap Wire" later in this chapter). Slide the wire onto the mandrel and use your fingers to press the wire down over the mandrel.

With smaller hoops, it is best to use a graduated mandrel, such as the graduated ring mandrel shown on the right. It enables you to perfect the round shape of the wire by sliding it up the mandrel as far as it will go.

With mandrels made of wood or metal, you can optionally use a rawhide hammer to tap the wire down against the mandrel to make shape adjustments. Use a chasing hammer when you also want to work-harden and texturize the wire.

HAMMER WIRE

You can use a hammer to work-harden, flatten, and texturize straight, bent, or shaped wire. To work-harden
wire without significantly changing its shape or texture,
tap lightly and repeatedly on the wire with a rawhide
hammer on top of a steel bench block.

To work-harden and flatten wire, you can use a chasing
hammer and steel bench block. Angle the hammer head
slightly downward so the edge that is farthest from you
is lower than the edge closest to you. Tap with the hammer moving slightly away from you.

You can texturize larger-gauge and flat wire by tapping
it lightly and evenly with the ball end of a ball peen or
chasing hammer.

TIP

How to hammer a shape that is not flat

When you hammer a shape that is not completely
flat, such as a hoop with a wrapped loop at the
top, place only the flat portion of the shape on
the bench block. When you hammer it, avoid
tapping the wire near the edge of the bench
block, which can mar the wire.

Make and Use Simple Connector Loops and Jump Rings

MAKE SIMPLE CONNECTOR LOOPS

You can use simple loops to connect wire components or attach charms or drops.

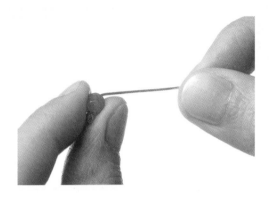

1. Bend back about ¼ inch of wire approximately 45 degrees. (In the example, the wire has been looped back on the opposite end to hold a bead and has not yet been cut to ¼ inch.) The bead provides leverage so that you can bend back the wire with your fingers. To begin making a loop on wire that does not have a bead, use flat nose pliers to make the bend.

2. Grasp the end of the wire with round nose pliers and rotate them away from you to make a loop.

3. If necessary, return the pliers to their starting position and roll the wire away from you again to complete the loop.

OPEN AND CLOSE SIMPLE CONNECTOR LOOPS

To open a simple wire loop, grasp it at an angle with chain nose or flat nose pliers, and bend it slightly to the side at its opening (a). To close the loop, use the same pliers to reverse this motion (b).

a

b

Basic Wirework *(continued)*

MAKE JUMP RINGS

Although you can save time by purchasing ready-made jump rings, you can make them yourself by using a pair of precision side cutters.

① Grasp the end of your wire with round nose pliers. The diameter of the pliers' jaws at the point where you grasp the wire dictates the inside diameter of your jump rings.

② Rotate the pliers to create a loop.

③ Remove the pliers from the wire and reinsert them into the loop in their original position.

④ Begin rolling the wire away from you again while using your thumb to position the new loop below the first loop on the pliers.

⑤ Continue using your thumb to guide the wire while using the pliers to make repeated coils at the same place on the jaws of the pliers. The coils will gradually move toward the tips of the pliers. Stop when you have one more coil than the number of jump rings you need.

⑥ Use side cutters to flush-cut the tip of the first coil.

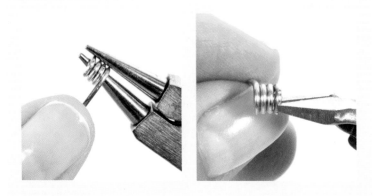

7 Turn the pliers around and make a flush-cut through the wire in the second coil. Align this cut with the first cut you made. The first jump ring should fall off the coil, and both of its ends should be flush.

8 Repeat steps 6–7 to cut each of the remaining jump rings.

OPEN AND CLOSE JUMP RINGS

It is important to open and close jump rings correctly to keep them from breaking or coming loose during wear.

To open a jump ring, hold it in front of you using two pairs of chain nose or flat nose pliers (or one of each), with the ring's opening facing upward. Gently twist one end of the ring toward you and the other end away from you.

To close a jump ring, twist the ends back in the opposite direction, and wiggle them together until the ring is completely closed. There should be no gap in the ring's opening.

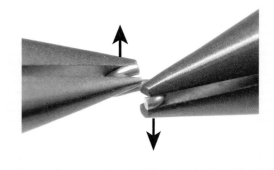

FAQ

How can I avoid marring wire with my pliers?

Over time, you should develop a feel for how much pressure to apply with your pliers to minimize scratches and dings. For most tasks, very gentle pressure is all that is needed. In the meantime, you can protect your wire by covering the jaws of your metal pliers with masking tape or electrical tape, or coating them with a product called Tool Magic, which is sold by jewelry making suppliers.

Wrap Wire

You can wrap wire around beads, other wire, or other jewelry components to create connections or add decorative elements to your designs.

Wrap Wire Over Wire

① Select a gauge of dead-soft wire that is smaller than the gauge of wire you want to wrap. The example uses 24-gauge over 18-gauge copper wire.

② Use flat nose pliers to bend the last ½ inch of smaller-gauge wire into a "U" shape.

③ Slide the shaped wire over the larger-gauge wire.

④ Using your thumb for leverage on the short wire tail, carefully wrap the long end all the way around the larger-gauge wire with your other hand.

⑤ Make a second wrap, working slowly and positioning this wrap up against the first.

⑥ Repeat this process to make as many wraps as you like.

⑦ Use side cutters to flush-cut both ends of the smaller gauge wire close to the wraps.

⑧ Use the tips of chain nose pliers to gently squeeze down both wire ends.

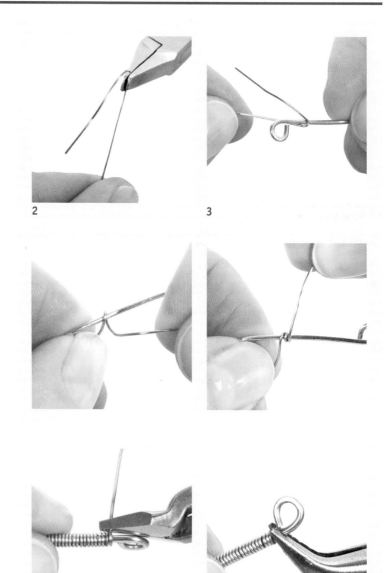

2

3

7

8

Wire Wrap Regular Beads

You can use wraps to secure wire loops at the ends of regular beads, which have holes drilled through their centers. In this example, a bead is strung onto wire that is looped back at the end.

1 Use round nose pliers to grasp the wire at the end of the bead.

2 Bend the rest of the wire to one side.

3 Reposition the pliers so that they grasp the wire just above the bend you just made.

4 Wrap the wire back over the pliers to create a loop.

5 Use chain nose or flat nose pliers to gently hold the loop closed and flat.

6 Use round nose or chain nose pliers (or, with longer lengths of wire, your fingers) to wrap the wire all the way around its base just below the loop.

7 Reposition the pliers at their starting position, and continue to make wraps down the base of the wire until it is completely covered with wraps.

8 Use side cutters to flush-cut the wire against the wraps.

9 If the wire end protrudes from the wraps, use the tips of chain nose pliers to squeeze it down.

2

3

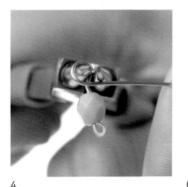

4

6

7

8

Wrap Wire *(continued)*

Wire Wrap a Briolette or Teardrop Bead

There are many ways to wrap loops on briolettes or teardrop beads to create decorative drops. Here is the technique used in this book:

1. Begin with a length of 26- or 24-gauge wire that is at least 10–12 inches long. (Larger beads require a little more wire.) The example uses 26-gauge bronze wire.

2. Pass the wire through the hole in the bead, and center the bead along the wire.

3. Bend both ends of the wire upward until they cross.

4

4. Uncross the wires and use your fingers to squeeze the wires together just past the tip of the bead.

5. Pull the wires through your fingers to straighten them, beginning at the point just above the small bends you made in Step 4.

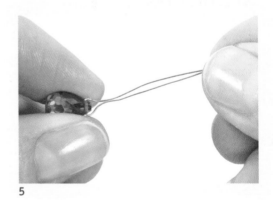

5

6. Grasp both wires with round nose pliers, just past the tip of the bead.

7. Bend both wires to one side over the pliers.

8. Reposition the pliers to just past the bend, and wrap both wires completely around the pliers to create a loop.

7   8

9 Wrap both wires around the base of the loop, taking care to keep them parallel to one another (do not allow them to cross). It's best to go slowly and keep the wraps a little bit loose; they do not need to be snug against the bead.

10 Continue wrapping down past the tip of the bead until you have your desired size of wrapped "cap."

11 Gently wrap just one of the wires once or twice around the cap toward the top loop. If the wire is getting short, complete this wrap using the tips of chain nose or round nose pliers.

12 Wrap the wire around the base of the loop at least once.

13 Use side cutters to flush-cut any excess wire close to the loop.

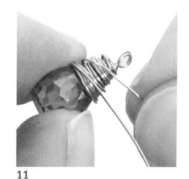

11

13

14 Gently wrap the second wire once or twice back up the cap toward the loop.

15 Wrap it around the base of the loop, on top of the first wire.

16 Use side cutters to flush-cut the second wire close to the loop.

17 Use the tips of chain nose pliers to gently squeeze down the wire ends.

15

17

Create a Patina with Liver of Sulfur

The best way to darken copper and copper-containing metals, such as sterling silver, is to oxidize them using a chemical called liver of sulfur. Liquid and gel formulations are the easiest to use. Be aware that although liver of sulfur is safe for most glass beads, it can alter the color of some gemstone beads and damage nonmetal components. Test it on a sample of those materials before oxidizing any completed design.

① Set up your work area in a well-ventilated location (preferably outdoors), put on latex gloves, and grab some paper towels in case of spills. (Liver of sulfur solution smells like rotten eggs, and its fumes are unhealthy to breathe.)

② Clean the wire component in soapy water or with rubbing alcohol. It is important to remove all oils from its surface.

③ Fill a small container with hot water. The water should be steaming, but not boiling. (Cooler water results in duller patina colors and lengthens the time it takes to create a patina.)

④ Following the directions on the liver of sulfur container or on your supplier's website, add a small amount of liver of sulfur to the water and allow it to dissolve. You usually need a smaller amount for copper and a larger amount for sterling silver or bronze.

⑤ Use tweezers or your gloved fingers to dunk the wire into the liver of sulfur solution and swish it around for a couple of seconds.

⑥ Remove the wire and rinse it well in clean water, either in a bowl or under a faucet.

2

5

6

7 Optionally, repeat steps 5–6 to create a darker patina. As the metal becomes more oxidized, the patina will turn from gold, to amber or brown, to red, to purple, to blue, to green, to gray, and finally to black.

8 Allow the wire to dry completely.

9 Optionally, brush the component lightly with fine steel wool to create a brushed finish.

9

After you finish, pour some baking soda into the liver of sulfur solution to neutralize it. When the fizzing stops, you can discard it down a drain (if approved by your local public works department) or into a bucket of cat litter to throw out with your regular trash.

The photo on the right shows patinated ear wires with beadwork added later (see "Stacked Bead Hoop Drops" in Chapter 5).

TIP

You can polish some wire with a jewelry polishing cloth

Use a jewelry polishing cloth to polish uncoated, solid metals such as sterling silver, brass, copper, and bronze. It brightens up the metal and can remove unwanted oxidation. If you apply a patina to your wire, polish it very lightly, if at all, to avoid removing the patina.

Although it's generally safe to polish gold- and silver-filled wire with a polishing cloth, avoid polishing plated metals. The light abrasive in the polishing cloth is often enough to wear through plating and expose the base metal.

Work with Chain

You can attach jewelry chain to earring components with jump rings. This section provides tips for working with chain efficiently.

Divide Open-Link Chain

Open links have cuts that enable you to open them with pliers.

① Lay the chain out straight beside a ruler, leaving about ¼ inch of space between the chain and the ruler.

② Locate the mark on the ruler that denotes your desired length, and press a finger against the chain on either side of the mark. (Doing so holds the chain taut.)

③ Use chain nose pliers to grasp the link that is 1 link past your measurement mark.

④ Release the chain from your fingers, and carefully lift it with the pliers.

⑤ Pick up a second pair of chain nose pliers, and use both pliers to twist each side of the link in opposite directions to open it.

⑥ Remove the length of chain. Use both pairs of pliers to close the open link by twisting the sides back toward each other.

Cut Closed-Link Chain

Closed links (sometimes called *soldered links*) do not have cuts. The only way to separate closed-link chain is to cut it and remove a link.

① Lay the chain out straight beside a ruler, leaving about ¼ inch of space between the chain and the ruler.

② Locate the link that is 1 link past the mark on the ruler for your desired length.

③ Use side cutters to cut carefully through the center of that link.

④ Remove the cut link with your fingers or chain nose pliers.

3

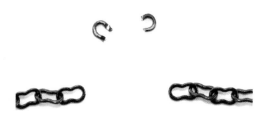

How can I keep the chain straight while making a cut?

Some chains are easier to lay out in a straight line if you first pin down their ends. Place the ruler and chain on corkboard (such as a bulletin board laid flat), and insert a sewing pin through the first link in the chain. The pin anchors the chain so that you can pull it straight alongside the ruler. Then pin down the other end of the chain a couple of inches past the link you want to cut.

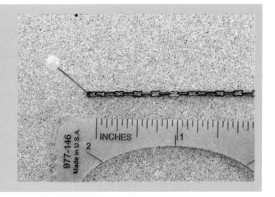

TIP

35

Beadwork

*B*eadwork involves stitching seed beads with sturdy thread. You can add interesting color and texture to earrings by incorporating beadwork into your designs. This section provides an overview of basic techniques and terminology used in this book. For in-depth coverage, see the book *Teach Yourself VISUALLY Beadwork*.

PULLING AND CUTTING BEADING THREAD

Begin by holding the spool of beading thread gently in one hand and the end of the thread in the other. Pull the end of the thread and the spool away from each other as far as your arms reach, allowing the spool to spin and release the thread. Use beading scissors to cut nylon beading thread (such as Nymo or C-Lon) and children's craft scissors, a hobby knife, or side cutters to cut the polyethylene thread called FireLine.

PRE-STRETCHING NYLON THREAD

Because nylon thread is prone to stretching, it's a good idea to pre-stretch it before you begin beading. Working in sections, hold the thread with your hands about 1 foot apart, and gently tug the thread in opposite directions. Do so for the entire length of thread. This step minimizes the risk that your beadwork will stretch out or sag over time.

WAXING OR CONDITIONING NYLON THREAD

When you buy unwaxed nylon beading thread, you should treat it with thread conditioner (such as Thread Heaven) to strengthen it, protect it from moisture, and make it less prone to tangling and stretching.

To apply conditioner, hold one end of the thread against the surface of the product, and slowly pull the entire length of thread through the product until the thread is fully coated. Go back and pull the thread between your finger and thumb to even out the coating. You can repeat this process as you stitch beads whenever it feels like the coating is wearing off.

THREADING A BEADING NEEDLE

Press the end of the thread between your fingers or fingernails to flatten it slightly. Hold the thread between the finger and thumb of your non-dominant hand, and use your dominant hand to slide the needle onto the thread.

POSITIONING THE NEEDLE

Most beadwork is performed by using a single strand of thread with the needle positioned several inches from the end and with the thread tail folded over. As you bead, keep the eye of the needle pressed between your finger and thumb to prevent the thread from slipping out.

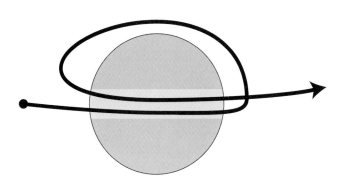

USING A STOP BEAD

Some projects begin by stringing a *stop bead* to keep the other beads on your thread. String a seed bead and position it 6–8 inches from the end of the thread. Pass the needle through it again in the same direction, and hold the bead while pulling the thread taut.

PICKING UP BEADS

When you *pick up* beads, you spear them with your needle. You can pick up one bead at a time, or stack beads on your needle in groups. You then slide them down onto your thread. For easy pickup, first pour your beads into ceramic dishes or into piles on a beading mat.

STITCHING BEADS

Always position your needle close to the inside upper surface of a bead hole. Slowly pull the thread through the bead, and then give the thread a few gentle tugs near the bead to make sure the thread is taut. If you make a mistake, unthread the needle and use it to pick out stitches.

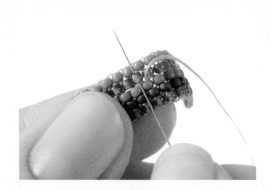

WEAVING-IN

You *weave-in* thread by passing the needle through beadwork that you have already completed, often making half hitch knots over existing thread along the way (see the next section). You can weave-in to hide a thread tail, begin a new length of thread mid-project, or simply reposition your needle.

MAKING HALF HITCH KNOTS

Make a *half hitch knot* in beadwork by passing your needle beneath the existing thread between two beads to create a small loop and then passing the needle through that loop from the other side. Pull the thread to cinch the knot.

USING A THREAD BURNER

You can use a *thread burner* to trim thread after you finish stitching. Pull the thread taut away from the beadwork, push the button on the burner, and touch its heating element to the thread close to the bead-work. Be very careful when using your thread burner, because its tip becomes red hot.

HOW TO READ A BEAD KEY

Project instructions often assign a capital letter to each color and size of bead used in a design. Together, these letters are referred to as a *bead key*. In this book, the bead key letters are shown in bold in the "Tools and Materials" sections of the projects that use beads. You might find it helpful to label your beads by their letters with slips of paper (a).

In project instructions, a number-letter combination is used to indicate which beads you need to pick up and string or stitch during a given step. For example, the beads in b were strung according to the following instructions, using the labeled beads from a:

- Pick up 2A, 2B, 2C, and 2D, and slide them down against the (black) stop bead.

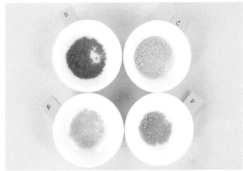

a

COMMON BEADWORK TERMS

The beadwork terms below are used throughout the beading projects in this book. Take a few moments to become familiar with them before you get started.

- **Pass through:** To stitch through a particular bead or group of beads.

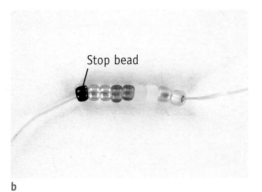

Stop bead

b

- **Pass back through:** To stitch through a bead or beads in the opposite direction that you passed through it (or them) the first time.

- **Thread path:** The route you take with your needle to stitch through existing beadwork.

- **Row:** A horizontal row of stitched beads.

- **Column:** A vertical column of stitched beads.

- **Round:** A row of beads in beadwork that is circular or curved.

How do I make a square knot in beading thread?

Square knots are often used to tie strung beads into circles or rings, or to secure two threads that exit the same bead. To make one, wrap the left strand around the right strand, and then wrap the right strand over and around the left strand. Pull both strands away from one another to tighten the knot.

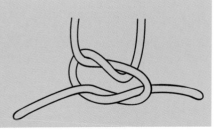

CHAPTER 3

Make Your Own Ear Wires

Ear wires are earring findings that slip through pierced ears. The most common styles that you can make yourself are French hooks, marquise wires, kidney wires, and hoops. There are many different ways to make them, and you might develop your own techniques over time. This chapter provides examples to help you get started.

Before you begin, be sure to review the following essential techniques from Chapter 2:

- "Straighten, Cut, and File Wire"
- "Bend, Shape, and Hammer Wire"
- "Make and Use Simple Connector Loops and Jump Rings"

French Hooks

French hooks are casual ear wires that are versatile and easy to make. This section covers the two styles of French hooks that are used in the projects in this book.

Bail-Maker French Hooks

This technique uses bail-making pliers (see "Wirework Supplies" in Chapter 1) to bend wire into simple French hooks.

1. Working with wire still on the spool, use nylon jaw pliers to straighten and stiffen several inches of wire. The example uses 20-gauge, dead-soft copper wire. (Be sure to read the precautions about copper wire in the section "Metal Type" in Chapter 2.)

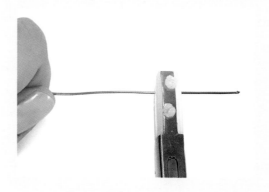

FAQ

What does it mean to work with wire "from the spool"?

When you work with wire directly from the spool, you start filing, bending, or shaping the wire before cutting it free from the spool or coil in which you purchased it. This technique helps conserve wire because you cut only as much wire as you need.

2 Use side cutters to flush-cut the tip of the wire.

3 Set your sliding brass gauge to the 1-inch mark, and hold it up next to the end of the wire.

4 Grasp the wire with your finger and thumb at the 1-inch mark.

2

3 and 4

5 Set down the brass gauge, and pick up your bail-making pliers.

6 Use the pliers to grasp the wire just above your thumb, with the larger barrel of the pliers facing away from you.

7 Use your other hand to bend the wire into a "U" around the larger barrel. (In the photo, the pliers have been flipped over.)

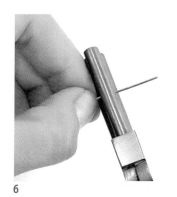

6

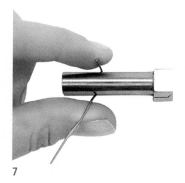

7

8 Use the bail-making pliers to slightly curl back the last ⅛ inch or so of wire.

9 Set the brass gauge to the ¼-inch mark, and hold it next to the straight portion of the wire just below the tip of the hook.

10 Grasp the wire with your finger and thumb next to the ¼-inch mark.

8

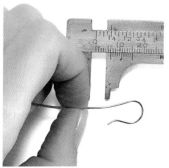

10

⑪ Use side cutters to flush-cut the wire just above your finger and thumb.

⑫ Set the ear wire aside, and repeat steps 1–8 to begin forming a second ear wire. Do your best to place your pliers on the wire and make the "U" the exact same way you did for the first ear wire.

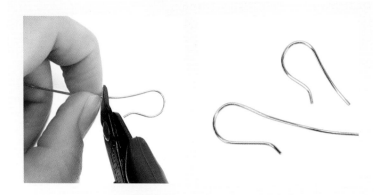

⑬ Stack the 2 ear wires, and use side cutters to flush-cut the second wire to the same length as the first.

NOTE: No two handmade ear wires are exactly the same size and shape; however, with practice you can learn to get them very close.

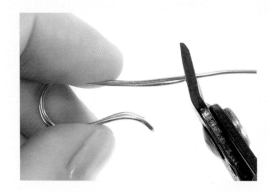

⑭ Use a needle file to flat-file the straight end and debur the curved end of each ear wire.

⑮ Grasp the straight end of each ear wire with round nose pliers, and bend each tip back to form a small loop (see the section "Bend Wire" in Chapter 2).

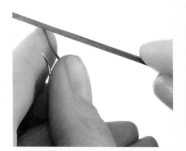

16 Place both ear wires on a steel bench block, and work-harden them with a rawhide hammer.

17 Use a chasing hammer to lightly flatten the upper portion of the large curve in each hoop.

18 If the hooks become slightly distorted, use your fingers to bend them back into shape.

16   17

19 To open the loop on each ear wire, use chain nose or flat nose pliers to twist it slightly to the side. (Bent chain nose pliers are shown in the example.)

20 Insert your earring drops and use flat nose pliers to gently twist each loop closed. If you choose bent chain nose pliers, you can use the backs of the jaws, as shown.

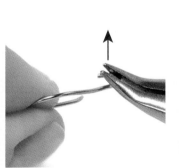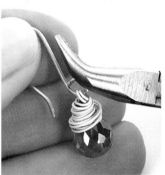

You now have a pair of handmade earrings, ready to wear. For drops, the completed earrings in the example have orange cubic zirconia briolettes wrapped with 26-gauge, egg white–colored copper wire. To learn how to make them, see the section "Wire Wrap a Briolette or Teardrop Bead" in Chapter 2.

Circular French Hooks

This style of French hook is more circular. The example uses 20-gauge, dead-soft copper wire.

1 Perform steps 1–2 of the section "Bail-Maker French Hooks."

2 Wrap the wire around a ½-inch (12mm) mandrel. This can be a mandrel designed for jewelry making, a piece of metal tubing, or even a permanent marker, as shown.

3 Adjust the wire so that it crosses on the back of the mandrel and overlaps by ¼ inch. In the example, a brass gauge is used to locate the ¼-inch mark. Alternatively, you can estimate this measurement.

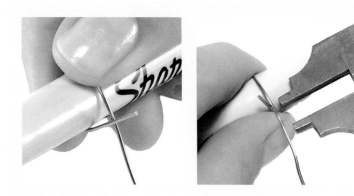

4 Use side cutters to flush-cut the spool end of the wire ¼ inch from where the wire crosses. In the example, thumb and finger are holding the wire at the pre-measured ¼-inch mark, and the wire has been slipped off of the mandrel to make the cut.

5 Set the trimmed loop of wire aside, and perform steps 1–2 again, using wire that is still on the spool. (To make sure you begin with a straight end, start by trimming the tip of the wire with a flush-cut.)

6 Slide both wire loops back onto the mandrel, and align them side by side.

7 Using the first loop as a guide, trim off the second loop with a flush-cut (a). Make the loops as close to identical as you can (b).

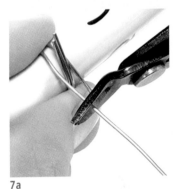

6

7a

8 Use a needle file to flat-file one end of each wire.

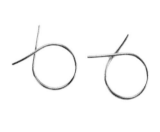

7b

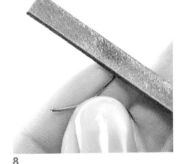

8

9 Use round nose pliers to curl those ends into small loops.

10 Use a needle file to debur the straight ends of the wires.

11 Use your fingers to gently open each wire so that the ends no longer cross.

9

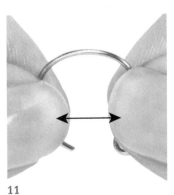

11

⑫ Pull the unlooped side of each wire slightly downward.

⑬ Use round nose pliers to gently bend back the straight end of each wire. Use the widest part of the pliers to make this bend.

⑭ Slide each ear wire back onto the mandrel, and use it and your fingers to gently bend the earrings into more circular shapes.

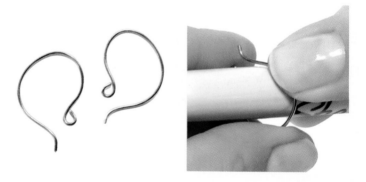

The ear wires after Step 13

⑮ Perform steps 16–20 of the section "Bail-Maker French Hooks" to work-harden, hammer, and complete your ear wires.

In the example, drops containing pairs of beads have been attached to the ear wires. The beads are 7mm x 5mm Czech fire-polished glass in copper fuchsia. They are strung on looped 20-gauge, dead-soft copper wire.

Marquise wires, which are sometimes called "V" wires, are shaped like marquise diamonds. They are more likely to hold their shape if you make them with half-hard (rather than dead-soft) wire. This example uses 22-gauge, half-hard sterling silver wire.

① Working with wire from the spool, run several inches of wire through the closed jaws of bracelet-bending pliers. Use the same technique you would use to straighten wire using flat nylon jaw pliers, but allow the wire to form a smooth curve.

② Use side cutters to flush-cut the tip of the wire.

③ Locate the place on the wire that is 1½ inches from the end. You can make this a straight, point-to-point measurement with a brass gauge, as shown.

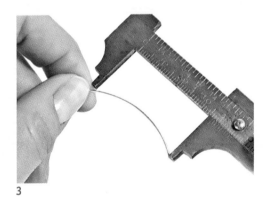

3

④ Grasp the wire with your finger and thumbnail at the 1½-inch mark.

⑤ Grasp the wire directly beside your finger and thumb with flat nose pliers.

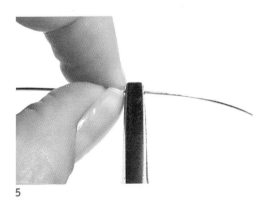

5

6 Use your thumb to push on the spool side of the wire just past the jaws of the pliers. Doing so creates what will be the "V" at the top of the marquise wires.

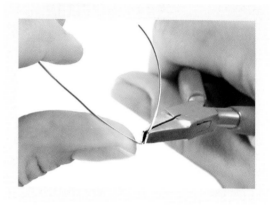

7 Trim the wire off of the spool by flush-cutting it about ¼ inch below the end of the wire, as shown.

8 Repeat steps 1–6 to begin the second ear wire.

9 Hold the first wire up against the second, and trim the second wire to the same length as the first.

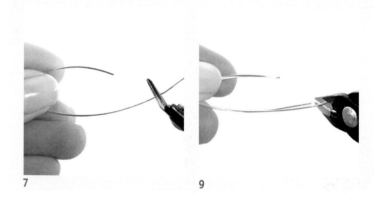

7

9

10 Use a needle file to flat-file the longer end and debur the shorter end of each wire.

11 Use round nose pliers to curl back the long end of each ear wire into a small loop.

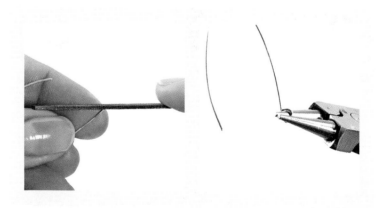

⑫ Place the wires on a steel bench block, and use a chasing hammer to slightly flatten their pointed tops.

⑬ To adjust the shape of each wire, gently squeeze its sides together until the ends cross.

⑭ Allow the ends to spring back open.

⑮ Attach your choice of drops to the completed marquise wires.

The marquise wires shown here are adorned with wrapped briolette drops (see the section "Wire Wrap a Briolette or Teardrop Bead" in Chapter 2). The briolettes are 10mm pale pink chalcedony gemstone.

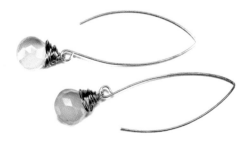

Bail-Maker Kidney Wires

Kidney wires are shaped like kidney beans. They're more secure to wear than French hooks or marquise wires because they come together and close at the bottoms. Like marquise wires, kidney wires are best made with half-hard wire. This example uses 22-gauge, half-hard, antiqued-bronze wire.

Basic Bail-Maker Kidney Wires

1 Working with wire from the spool, run several inches of wire through the closed jaws of flat nylon jaw pliers.

2 Use side cutters to flush-cut the tip of the wire.

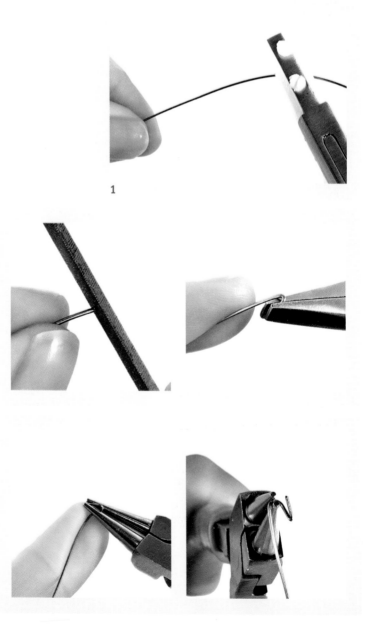

1

3 Use a needle file to flat-file the end of the wire.

4 Grasp the end of the wire with flat nose pliers, and use them to make a sharp "V"-shaped bend. The length of wire you bend back should be approximately equal to the width of your pliers' jaws.

5 Grasp the "V" with round nose pliers, and use them and your finger to bend the "V" 90 degrees, as shown.

6 Move the round nose pliers down to below the "V" and bend back the wire to create an upside-down "U."

7 Reposition the pliers, as shown, and make a loop just to the side of the "U." Bring the wire all the way around the pliers, in the direction indicated by the arrow.

8 Reposition the pliers again, and bend back the wire in the opposite direction.

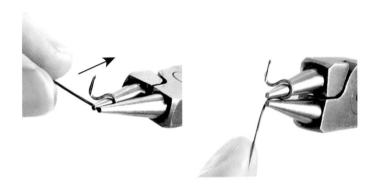

9 Check to make sure that the wire looks like the photo on the right. This completes the bottom loop and latch mechanism on the kidney wire.

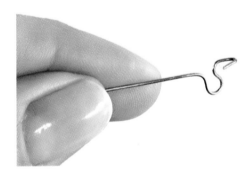

10 Grasp the wire with your finger and thumbnail about 1 inch down from the bottom loop you just made.

11 Grasp the wire with bail-making pliers against your finger and thumbnail. Position the pliers so that the smaller barrel is below the wire, as shown.

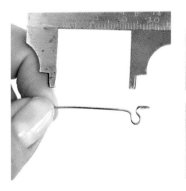

⑫ Bend the spool side of the wire all the way around the larger barrel of the bail-making pliers until the wire crosses.

⑬ Trim the spool end of the wire about ¼ inch below the bottom loop, as shown.

⑭ Repeat steps 1–12 to begin the second kidney wire.

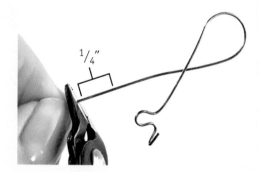

⑮ Stack and align the 2 wires side by side, and flush-cut the second wire to the same length as the first.

⑯ Use your fingers to gently pull the sides of each kidney wire in opposite directions to uncross them.

⑰ Grasp the straight end of each wire with the bail-
making pliers, with the larger barrel facing outward.

⑱ Use the bail-making pliers to gently curl back each
wire.

⑲ Use a needle file to debur each end.

⑳ Latch each kidney wire by placing the curved end
behind the bend that you made in Step 6.

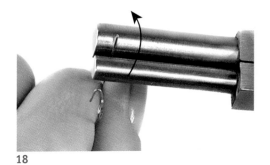

18

㉑ Use your fingers to gently pull
the sides of each kidney wire in
opposite directions to adjust
their shapes.

㉒ Use your fingers and thumbs to
slightly widen the curve at the top
of each kidney wire.

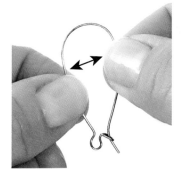 

㉓ Unlatch each kidney hook, and pull the sides of each
ear wire in opposite directions (like you did in Step
21) until the bottom ends are about ¾ inch apart.

㉔ If needed, use your fingers and (optionally) bail-
making pliers or flat nose pliers to perfect the shape
and curve of each kidney wire. Grasp and gently
bend or straighten the wire anywhere it looks
uneven or improperly curved.

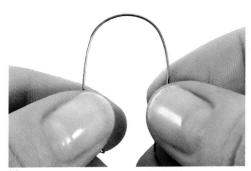

23

㉕ Using a steel bench block and chasing hammer, lightly hammer the top of each kidney wire.

㉖ To attach drops to your kidney wires, slide the drops into the bottom loops when the kidney wires are unlatched. The drops in the example are vintage pressed-glass beads, stacked on antiqued-brass head pins and secured with wrapped top loops (see the section "Wrap Wire" in Chapter 2).

25

㉗ Squeeze the upper sides of each loop together with round nose pliers to help keep your drops from slipping out. Your kidney wire earrings are now ready to wear. However, you can make the drops more secure and add decorative accents by wrapping the top of each bottom loop, as shown in the next section.

Wrapped-Loop Bail-Maker Kidney Wires

➊ After making your basic bail-maker kidney wires, use flat nylon jaw pliers to straighten several inches of 24-gauge, dead-soft wire. The example uses bronze-finish copper craft wire.

➋ Trim off about 2 inches of the 24-gauge wire.

➌ Use flat nose pliers to bend the wire into a "V" near its middle.

3

④ Slide the wire "V" all the way over the top of one of the bottom loops, back to front (that is, with the ends of the "V" extending out from the front of the earring, as shown).

⑤ Bend one side of the "V" back and over the top of the kidney wire loop.

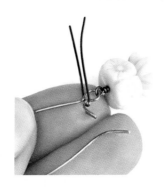

⑥ Turn the kidney wire over and bend the other side of the "V" back and over the kidney wire loop.

⑦ Use side cutters to flush-cut each end of the "V" wire close to the wraps that you just made.

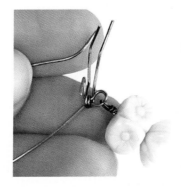

⑧ Use chain nose pliers to squeeze down the ends that you just trimmed.

⑨ Repeat steps 1–8 to complete the second ear wire in your pair.

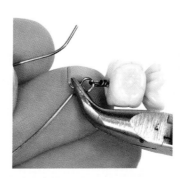

Beading hoops are hoops of wire that latch at the top with a simple loop closure. They hold their shape best when you make them with half-hard (rather than dead-soft) wire. This example uses 22-gauge, half-hard, antiqued-bronze wire.

1. Working with wire still on the spool, run several inches of wire through the closed jaws of flat nylon jaw pliers.

2. Use side cutters to flush-cut the tip of the wire.

3. Use a needle file to flat-file the end of the wire.

4. Wrap the wire around a mandrel the size of your choice. A 1¼-inch (30mm) wooden dowel is used in the example. (This step takes a little more effort with half-hard wire than it does with dead-soft wire.)

4

5. Position the wire so that it overlaps by about ¼ inch on the back of the mandrel.

6. While holding the wire against the mandrel with one hand, use the finger and thumb of your other hand to grasp the spool end of the wire a matching ¼ inch down from where the wire crosses.

6

7. Use side cutters to flush-cut the wire at that ¼-inch point.

8. Remove the wire from the mandrel, and repeat steps 1–4 to begin a second hoop.

9. Remove the second wire from the mandrel, and allow it to spring open.

10. Stack and align the first and second wires, and flush-cut the second wire to the same length as the first.

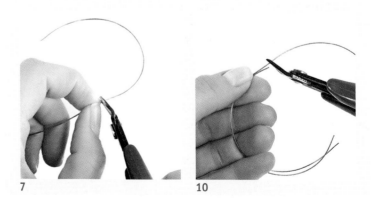

7

10

⑪ Use a needle file to flat-file the newly trimmed ends of each hoop.

⑫ Use round nose pliers to form a small sideways loop on one end of each hoop wire.

⑬ Grasp one small loop with flat nose pliers, and bend it slightly downward toward the inside of the hoop. Repeat this step for the second hoop.

⑭ Grasp the straight end of one hoop with flat nose pliers. Position the pliers so that the edge of the jaws aligns with the end of the wire, as shown.

⑮ Bend the wire upward a full 90 degrees. (This angle ensures that the ear wires do not come unlatched too easily).

⑯ Repeat steps 14–15 on the second hoop.

⑰ Use your fingers to gently bend and shape each hoop as necessary to correct its shape. You can make your hoops circular or teardrop shaped.

⑱ Optionally, use a bench block and chasing hammer to hammer the entire hoop portion of the ear wires, or just the bottoms of the hoops.

⑲ To latch the ear wires, simply slide the bent end of the wire through the loop on the opposite end.

You can wear your hoops unadorned, attach beaded drops, or wrap beads onto the hoop frames. In the example on the right, multiple lengths of Vintaj 5mm brass chain have been slipped onto each hoop.

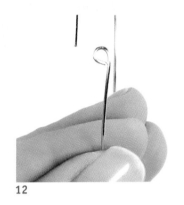
12

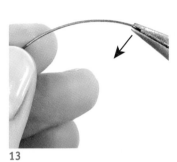
13

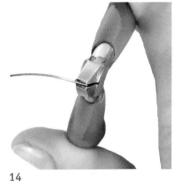
14

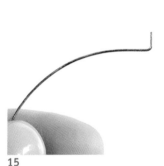
15

Drop Hoops

Drop hoops are wire frames that you attach to ear wires. They have more movement than basic beading hoops and are a good option when you want to use dead-soft (instead of half-hard) wire. This example uses 20-gauge, dead-soft bronze wire.

1 Perform steps 1–13 of "Beading Hoops." In this example, a spice jar is used as a mandrel.

NOTE: To adorn your hoops, you can string beads onto the wire before performing Step 2. See the completed earrings at the end of this section for an example.

2 Grasp the straight end of one hoop with flat nose pliers. Position the pliers about ½ inch from the end of the wire.

3 Use the pliers to bend the wire upward 90 degrees.

4 Slide the bent part of the wire up through the loop on the opposite side.

5 Use the flat nose pliers to bend back the wire another 45 degrees, as shown.

6 Use round nose pliers to roll that portion of the wire forward into a loop.

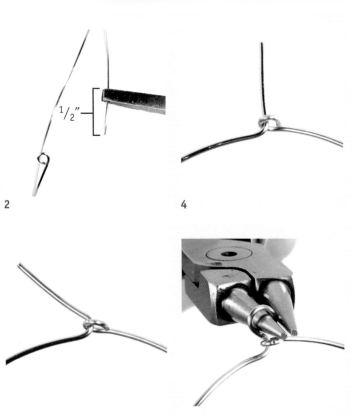

7 Repeat steps 2–6 with the other hoop wire.

8 Use your fingers to gently bend and shape each hoop as necessary to correct its shape. You can make your hoops circular or teardrop shaped.

9 Optionally, use a bench block and chasing hammer to hammer the entire hoop portion of the ear wires, or just the bottoms of the hoops.

10 Use flat nose pliers to attach your hoops to ear wires by opening and closing the loops on the hoops, or the loops on the ear wires. You can use any style of ear wire from this chapter, or a ready-made ear wire of your choice.

You can wear your hoops unadorned, attach beaded drops, or wrap beads onto the hoop frames. In the example on the right, nine 4mm lava rock beads were strung onto the hoops before completing Step 2. The ear wires are from the section "Circular French Hooks."

TIP

Other ways to connect the tops of drop hoops

There are many different approaches to securing the tops of drop hoops. In the example on the left (a), both ends of the hoop have been looped back with round nose pliers and a jump ring inserted between them. The ready-made ear wire is attached with a second jump ring inserted through the first.

In the example on the right (b), one end of the hoop is looped with round nose pliers, and chain nose pliers were used to wrap the other end around the frame twice.

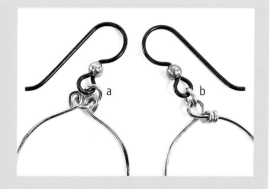

CHAPTER 4

Long and Linear

The earrings in this chapter are long, narrow, and sleek. They feature links, wraps, and bead weaving.

Beaded Chain Earrings

Beaded chains are simple designs that make surprisingly elegant earrings.

Specifications

Estimated time to complete: 35 minutes ● **Approximate length:** 4 inches

TECHNIQUES

Chapter 2

- "Pulling and Cutting Beading Thread"
- "Open and Close Simple Connector Loops"
- "Making Half Hitch Knots"
- "Pre-Stretching Nylon Thread"
- "Waxing or Conditioning Nylon Thread"
- "Threading a Beading Needle"
- "Using a Stop Bead"

- "Picking Up Beads"
- "Stitching Beads"
- "Weaving-In"
- "How to Read a Bead Key"
- "Common Beadwork Terms"

Chapter 3

- "Bail-Maker French Hooks"

TOOLS AND MATERIALS

- Size B nylon beading thread in black

- Beading scissors

- Thread conditioner

- Size 12 beading needle

- Bead mat and (optional) bead dishes (for pouring out beads)

- 0.4 grams of size 15/0 Miyuki round seed beads in opaque black (**A**)

- 18 Preciosa Twin beads in opaque black (**B**)*

- 2 Miyuki 5mm Tila beads in matte metallic gold or bronze (**C**)*

- 16 size 8/0 Miyuki round seed beads in opaque black (**D**)

- 6 Miyuki or Toho 3mm magatama beads in opaque black (**E**)

- 1 size 11/0 round seed bead to use as a stop bead

- About 4 inches of 20-gauge, dead-soft, round red brass wire

- Ruler (for measuring thread)

- Side cutters; flat nylon jaw pliers; bail-making pliers; brass gauge; medium-cut, flat needle file; round nose pliers; chasing hammer; steel bench block; and flat nose pliers (all for making and attaching ear wires)

*Look for Tila and Twin beads (as well as regular seed beads) at http://store.goodybeads.com. For the Twin beads, search for "Czech twin seed beads."

Make the Beaded Chain Earrings

1. Use beading scissors to cut a 2½-foot length of beading thread.

2. Gently pre-stretch the thread and condition it with thread conditioner.

3. Thread the needle, and fold over a tail of about 5–6 inches.

4. String the stop bead (red in the example), and secure it about 8 inches from the end of the thread.

5. Pick up 2A, 1B, 1A, 1C, and 1A and slide them down to the stop bead. (See the section "Tools and Materials" for the bead key.)

6. Pick up 7 sets of the following sequence of beads, and slide them down on the thread: 1B, 2A, 1D, and 2A.

7. Pick up 1B, 1A, 3E, and 1A, and slide them down.

5

6

8. Pass back up through the empty hole in the last B in the strand, and pull the thread gently taut.

9. Pick up 2A and pass back through the next D in the strand.

10. Hold the beads between your fingers and pull the thread gently taut again.

8

9

⑪ Repeat the following sequence until you arrive back at the top end of the strand, just below the C and the A right before it: Pick up 2A, pass through the next D, pick up 2A, pass through the empty hole in the next B, and pull the thread gently taut.

⑫ Pick up 1A and pass up through the empty hole in the C.

⑬ Pick up 1A and pass up through the empty hole in the last B.

11

⑭ Pick up 2A and 1D, and pull the thread gently taut.

⑮ Remove the needle, and use it to slide off the stop bead.

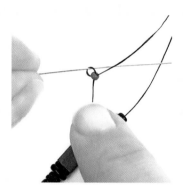

FAQ

How can I avoid overly loose thread tension?

If bare thread shows through noticeably between beads in your beadwork, your thread tension is too loose. While beading, stop occasionally and give the thread a few tugs to cinch it up. With thin thread (such as size B thread) and large-hole beads (such as Twin beads), you need to do so more often than with thicker thread and beads with smaller holes. Keep in mind that managing thread tension becomes easier with practice.

16 Thread the needle on the thread tail that previously held the stop bead.

17 Hold the last D in the beadwork between your finger and thumb, and pass up through that D with the needle and thread.

18 Pull both thread tails gently to adjust the tension on the thread within the beadwork. Try to eliminate any noticeable spaces between beads, but do not pull so tightly that the beadwork curls.

19

19 Tie a square knot just above the last D in the bead-work (see the FAQ "How do I make a square knot in beading thread?" in Chapter 2).

20 Pick up 7A and slide them down against the D.

21 Pass back down through the D and through the next 2A, 1B, and 1A in the beadwork.

22 Pull the thread gently taut, and then make a half hitch knot over the thread running between the beads.

23 Tug the thread a few times to pull down the knot and cinch up the tension in the beaded top loop.

21

22

24 Pass through several more beads, pull the thread gently taut again, and tie another half hitch knot.

25 Repeat steps 22–24 at least twice more to finish weaving-in the thread.

26 Pass through several more beads, and then cut the thread close to the beadwork.

26

27. Thread the needle on the remaining thread tail.

28. Pass up through the entire 7-bead loop at the end of the beadwork, following the same path you used with the other thread tail. Stitch through several beads at a time, keeping the thread pulled taut.

29. Weave-in this thread tail the same way you did the first: Pass through several beads, make a half hitch knot, and so on.

30. Cut the thread close to the beadwork.

29

31. Repeat steps 1–30 to create the beadwork for a second earring.

32. Use 20-gauge brass wire to make a pair of Bail-Maker French Hooks. Be sure to make the end loops on your ear wires large enough to hold the beaded end loops on your beadwork.

33. Attach the ear wires to the beaded top loops on your beadwork to complete the earrings.

33

Clover Kite Earrings

These colorful earrings are surprisingly simple to make.

Specifications

Estimated time to complete: 40 minutes ● **Approximate length:** 4¼ inches

TECHNIQUES

Chapter 2

- "Straighten Wire"
- "Cut Wire"
- "Bend, Shape, and Hammer Wire"

- "Make Simple Connector Loops"
- "Open and Close Simple Connector Loops"

Chapter 3

- "Bail-Maker French Hooks"

TOOLS AND MATERIALS

- 6 brass, 20- or 21-gauge, 1½-inch ball-end head pins
- 2 carved, dyed yellow magnesite, 17mm clover flower beads (available in multicolor strands)*
- 14 faceted grade AA 4mm aqua amazonite beads*
- About 20 inches of 22-gauge, red brass, dead-soft, round wire
- About 4 inches of 20-gauge, red brass, dead-soft, round wire

- Sliding brass gauge and ruler
- Fine-tip permanent marker
- Side cutters
- Round nose and flat nose pliers
- Flat nylon jaw pliers
- Bail-making pliers, chasing hammer, and steel bench block (for making ear wires)

*Look for these at www.beadaholique.com.

Make the Clover Kite Earrings

① Slide one of the head pins through one of the drilled holes in a clover flower, with the ball end of the head pin on the inside of the flower.

② Use your fingers to hold the ball end of the head pin against the inside edge of the flower, and bend the head pin 45 degrees on the outside of the flower.

2

③ Use side cutters to flush-cut the head pin just a little over ¼ inch from the outside edge of the flower. (Remember to aim the notched side of the pliers away from you to protect your eyes.)

④ Use the tips of round nose pliers to curl the wire into a loop.

⑤ Repeat steps 1–4 to add a connector loop to the other end of the flower bead.

⑥ Use flat nose pliers to neaten the loops and wiggle their ends closed.

⑦ Use a permanent marker to mark your round nose pliers at the place where their jaws are about 1½mm in diameter. (The mark will wear off over time.) Use a sliding brass gauge to locate the 1½mm mark.

3

6

⑧ Use flat nylon jaw pliers to straighten and work-harden several inches of 22-gauge wire still on the spool, and trim the end with a flush-cut.

⑨ String an amazonite bead onto the wire.

⑩ Grasp the end of the wire with round nose pliers, aligning the wire with the mark.

⑪ Roll the end of the wire into a loop.

⑫ Slide the bead up against the loop, and bend the wire below it 45 degrees. Do this in the opposite direction that you rolled the first loop.

12

⑬ Use side cutters to flush-cut the wire about ¼ inch below the bead.

⑭ Use round nose pliers to roll the trimmed wire into a loop.

⑮ Use flat nose pliers to neaten up both loops on the bead, and to open one of the loops.

⑯ Slide the open loop into one of the loops on a flower, and close it to connect the bead and the flower.

16

⑰ Trim off the tip of the 22-gauge wire on the spool with a flush-cut.

⑱ Repeat steps 8–15 to make a second bead link.

⑲ Use flat nose pliers to connect one loop on this bead link with the empty loop on the first bead link.

⑳ Continue adding bead links until you have a total of 6 linked beads connected to the flower. (Pull and straighten more wire on the spool to work with as necessary.)

20

㉑ String an amazonite bead onto a head pin, and slide it down against the ball end.

㉒ Grasp the bead with flat nylon jaw pliers for leverage, and bend the head pin 45 degrees.

㉓ Flush-cut the head pin a little over ¼ inch from the bead, and use round nose pliers to roll the wire into a loop.

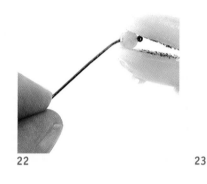

22   23

㉔ Use flat nose pliers to neaten the loop and connect it to the empty loop on the sixth linked bead.

㉕ Repeat steps 1–6 and 8–24 to make a second flower with a total of 7 linked 4mm beads.

㉖ Use 20-gauge wire to make a pair of Bail-Maker French Hooks.

㉗ Use flat nose pliers to attach the empty loop on each flower to an ear wire.

24   27

Because the clover flower beads are sold in multicolor strands, you can make more earrings in different color combinations. The earrings on the right were made with 4mm round amethyst (a) and 5mm yellow jade rondelle (b) beads.

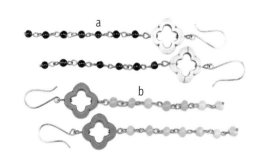

a

b

Just be aware that lower-quality gemstone beads can have smaller holes than higher-quality beads of the same size. If you find beads with holes too small to accommodate the 22-gauge wire or the head pins, you can use a smaller gauge (such as 24-gauge) and secure the beads with wrapped links rather than simple links (see the section "Wire Wrap Regular Beads" in Chapter 2).

Silver Archer Earrings

The curved lines of these post earrings are reminiscent of miniature archer's bows.

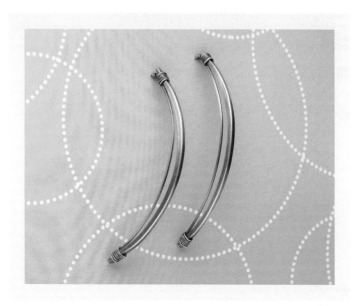

Specifications

Estimated time to complete: 40 minutes ● **Approximate length:** 2 inches

TECHNIQUES
Chapter 2

- "Straighten, Cut, and File Wire"

- "Bend, Shape, and Hammer Wire"

- "Make Simple Connector Loops"

- "Open and Close Simple Connector Loops"

Chapter 3

- "Bail-Maker French Hooks"

TOOLS AND MATERIALS

- 6 inches of 14-gauge, dead-soft, square sterling silver wire

- 7 inches of 20-gauge, half-hard, square sterling silver wire

- 20 inches of 26-gauge, dead-soft, round sterling silver wire

- Flat nylon jaw pliers

- Ruler or sliding brass gauge (for measuring wire)

- Steel bench block and chasing hammer

- Medium-cut, flat needle file

- Larger side cutters (suitable for 14-gauge wire)

- Bracelet-bending pliers

- Masking tape

- Liver of sulfur, rubber gloves, water, paper towels, and fine steel wool (for creating a patina)

- Ready-made sterling silver post earring backs

Make the Silver Archer Earrings

1 Run 6 inches of 14-gauge square wire through the jaws of flat nylon jaw pliers to straighten it.

2 Use side cutters to flush-cut two 2½-inch lengths of the 14-gauge wire. To ensure that they are the same length, you can use the first cut wire as a measuring guide for the second.

2

3 One at a time, place each wire on your bench block, and use a chasing hammer to slightly flatten both ends.

4 Use the needle file to smooth the jagged ends of both wires.

5 Use bracelet-bending pliers to bend each wire into a curve. Starting at one end, grasp the wire with the pliers and squeeze the handles together firmly (a). Then reposition the pliers about ½ inch down the wire, and squeeze the handles together again. Repeat this process for the entire length of each wire (b).

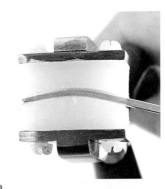 

a   b

6. Use flat nylon jaw pliers to straighten about 7 inches of 20-gauge, half-hard, square wire.

7. Flush-cut two 3-inch lengths of the 20-gauge wire.

8. Use flat nose pliers to make a 45-degree bend ½ inch from the end of each wire.

9. Use the needle file to debur the ends that are bent 45 degrees.

8

10. Use bracelet-bending pliers to curve the 20-gauge wire the same way you curved the 14-gauge wire, but do *not* curve the bent ½ inch of each wire. Make the curve in the same direction that you made that bend.

11. Press one of the 14-gauge wires and one of the 20-gauge wires together, with the thinner wire inside the curve of the thicker wire, and the 45-degree bend in the thinner wire aligned with one end of the thicker wire.

12. Use a small piece of masking tape to hold the 2 wires together near the bend, as shown.

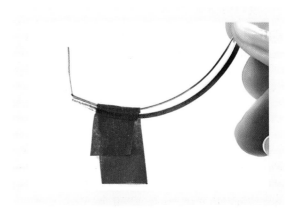

13. Use your fingers to gently straighten about 4 inches of 26-gauge round wire.

14. Use flat nose pliers to make a "U" about 1 inch from one end of the 26-gauge wire. Slide it over the stacked 14- and 20-gauge wires near the untaped ends, and make several tight wraps around both wires.

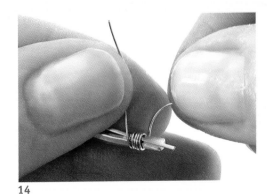

14

15. After 5 or 6 wraps, use side cutters to trim the wire close to the wraps on the inside of the curve, as shown.

16. Use the tips of chain nose pliers to neaten the wraps and press down each end of the 26-gauge wire.

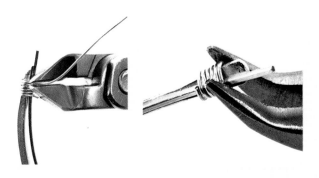

17. Cut and gently straighten a 6-inch length of 26-gauge wire.

18. Remove the masking tape from the stacked wires, and use the new 26-gauge wire to make 5 or 6 tight wraps around the 14- and 20-gauge wires near the bend at the top. Be sure to wrap in a direction going toward the bend (upward), and not away from it.

NOTE: It is important to make these wraps very tight, and to make the final wrap as close to the bend in the 20-gauge wire as possible. Doing so ultimately keeps the 20-gauge wire from sliding down.

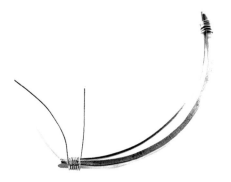

18

⑲ Bring the 26-gauge wire under and then up around the bent portion of the 20-gauge wire, near where it rests against the 14-gauge wire.

⑳ Make 2 wraps around the 20-gauge wire.

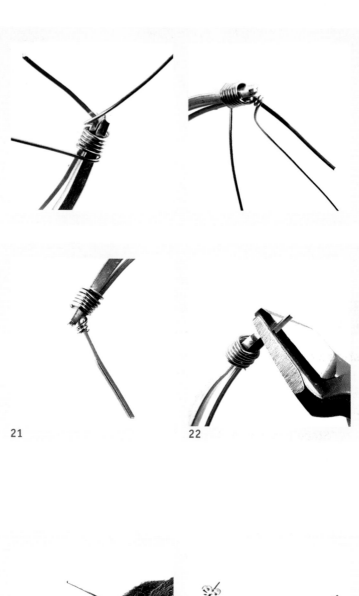

㉑ Trim both ends of the wire, and use the tips of chain nose pliers to neaten the wraps and to press down the wire ends.

㉒ Go back to the other end of the stacked wires and use side cutters to flush-cut the overlapping 20-gauge wire so that it is even with the end of the 14-gauge wire.

㉓ Use the needle file to gently smooth the jagged edge of the 20-gauge wire. (It is fine if you refile the end of the 14-gauge wire at the same time.)

21

22

㉔ Repeat steps 11–23 on the second pair of 14-gauge and 20-gauge wires to make a second earring.

㉕ Use liver of sulfur to create a dark patina on the earrings and then brush them lightly with fine steel wool (see the section "Create a Patina with Liver of Sulfur" in Chapter 2).

㉖ Slide an earring back onto each post to complete your earrings.

25

26

Art Glass Wand Earrings

M ake these artsy earrings by wrapping beads over wire.

Specifications

Estimated time to complete: 1 hour ● **Approximate length:** 3½ inches

TECHNIQUES

Chapter 2

- "Straighten, Cut, and File Wire"

- "Bend, Shape, and Hammer Wire"

- Optional: "Create a Patina with Liver of Sulfur"

- "Make Simple Connector Loops"

- "Open and Close Simple Connector Loops"

- "Wrap Wire Over Wire"

Chapter 3

- "Bracelet-Bender Marquise Wires"

TOOLS AND MATERIALS

- 4 inches of 18-gauge, dead-soft, round sterling silver wire

- 30 inches of 24-gauge, dead-soft, round sterling silver wire

- 9 inches of 22-gauge, half-hard, square sterling silver wire

- Sliding brass gauge or ruler (for measuring wire)

- Side cutters

- Flat nylon jaw pliers

- Medium-cut, flat needle file

- Round nose and flat nose pliers

- Steel bench block, chasing hammer, and raw-hide hammer

- About 0.85 grams of size 11/0 Delica cylinder beads in spring flowers color mix

- Beading mat and/or bead dishes

- Bracelet-bending pliers

Make the Art Glass Wand Earrings

1. Use flat nylon jaw pliers to straighten several inches of 18-gauge wire that is still on the spool.

2. Use side cutters to trim the tip of the wire with a flush-cut.

3. Cut a 2-inch length of wire, also making a flush-cut.

4. Repeat steps 1–3 to make a second 2-inch length of wire. You can use the first wire as a measuring guide.

4

5. If necessary, use flat nylon jaw pliers to gently bend each wire until it is relatively straight.

6. Use a needle file to flat-file both ends of each wire.

7. Use round nose pliers to make a small loop at one end of each wire.

8. One at a time, place each wire on your bench block and use a chasing hammer to lightly hammer the loop and the straight end.

7

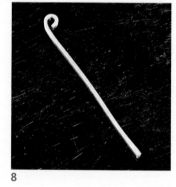

8

9. Hammer the entire lengths of both wires with a rawhide hammer on the bench block.

10. Use flat nose pliers to gently squeeze the loop at the end of each wire closed.

11. Use the needle file to smooth the edges of the straight end of each wire.

10

11

⑫ Pull and cut 15 inches of 24-gauge wire, and run it gently through your fingers to straighten it.

⑬ Use the technique from the section "Wrap Wire Over Wire" in Chapter 2 to begin wrapping the 24-gauge wire over one of the 18-gauge wires, close to the end loop. Begin with a couple of loose "starter" wraps, and then make 3 tight wraps.

⑭ Unwrap the starter wraps, and slide the 3 tight wraps up against the loop.

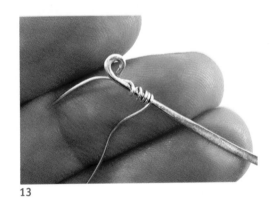

13

⑮ Using the loose end of the 24-gauge wire like a needle, pick up and string 12 cylinder beads in random order, and slide them down against the wraps.

⑯ Holding the loop at the end of the 18-gauge wire and the 24-gauge wire tail together for leverage, slowly wrap the beaded wire around the 18-gauge wire until all 12 beads are against the 18-gauge wire.

16

⑰ Wrap the 24-gauge wire around the 18-gauge wire 3 times, stacking the wraps tightly against one another.

⑱ String another set of 12 cylinder beads, and slide them down against the wraps.

⑲ Wrap them around the 18-gauge wire. At this point, you can turn the 18-gauge wire by its loop (as if it were a key) to help you make the wraps.

17

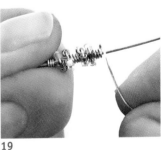

19

㉑ Repeat this process (wrapping 12 beads and making 3 wire wraps) 4 or 5 more times, for a total of 6 or 7 clusters of wrapped beads. The example earrings have 7 clusters.

㉑ For the final wraps, make a total of 6 or 7 wraps (rather than the usual 3).

Final wraps

21

㉒ Use side cutters to trim both wire tails close to the wraps at either end of the wire.

㉓ Use the tips of chain nose pliers to squeeze down the wire ends.

NOTE: If the ends feel sharp, you can file them with a needle file.

㉔ Repeat steps 12–23 to wrap beads around the second piece of 18-gauge wire.

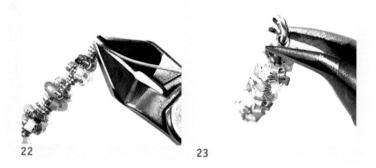

22   23

㉕ Use square 22-gauge wire to make a pair of Bracelet-Bender Marquise Wires.

㉖ Attach the marquise wires to the top loops on your bead-wrapped wands to complete the earrings.

If you'd like, you can use liver of sulfur to create a dark patina (not shown) on your completed earrings (see the section "Create a Patina with Liver of Sulfur" in Chapter 2). When they are dry, you can brush them lightly with a piece of fine steel wool. Tear off a narrow piece of the wool to use on the wraps between clusters of beads.

Segmented Rondelle Earrings

H ammered segments of wire give these earrings a sleek, linear look.

Specifications

Estimated time to complete: 1 hour ● **Approximate length:** 3 inches

TECHNIQUES

Chapter 2

- "Straighten, Cut, and File Wire"
- "Hammer Wire"
- "Make Jump Rings"
- "Open and Close Simple Connector Loops"

- "Open and Close Jump Rings"
- "Wire Wrap Regular Beads"
- "Wire Wrap a Briolette or Teardrop Bead"

Chapter 3

- "Circular French Hooks"

TOOLS AND MATERIALS

- About 2½ inches of 16-gauge, dead-soft, round bronze wire
- About 30 inches of 26-gauge, dead-soft, round bronze wire
- About 4 inches of 20-gauge, dead-soft, round bronze wire
- Side cutters
- Ruler or sliding brass gauge
- 1.25mm round hole-punching pliers

- Medium-cut, flat needle file
- Chain nose pliers
- Jewelry polishing cloth
- Fine steel wool
- 8 cubic zirconia 4mm faceted rondelle beads in dark Siam red
- Chasing hammer and steel bench block
- Mandrel and flat nylon jaw pliers
- Optional: Flat nose pliers

Segmented Rondelle Earrings *(continued)*

Make the Segmented Rondelle Earrings

① Working from the spool, use nylon jaw pliers to straighten at least 2½ inches of 16-gauge wire.

② Use side cutters to trim the end of the wire so that it is flush.

③ Use a ruler or sliding brass gauge to measure 1 inch of wire, and cut off that inch with a flush-cut.

④ Trim the end of the wire on the spool so that it is flush.

⑤ Using the inch-long segment of wire as a measuring guide, flush-cut another inch-long segment of wire.

5

⑥ Make sure that both segments are relatively straight. You can use nylon jaw pliers to adjust them.

⑦ Hold down a segment on your bench block, and use a chasing hammer in the other hand to flatten the opposite end of the segment. Pound on the wire with the center of the hammer head, and move the hammer slightly away from the wire as it touches down.

⑧ Hammer this end of the segment until it is wide enough to more than cover the hole on the bottom of your hole-punching pliers. Make the flattened ends as wide as you reasonably can to ensure that they are large enough to accommodate a hole (see Step 12).

NOTE: Depending on the structure of your work table, this hammering may be loud. If it bothers you, wear earplugs or protective ear muffs.

⑨ Turn the wire around, and repeat this process on the other end.

8

⑩ Gently tap the middle of one side of the segment with the chasing hammer to flatten it slightly and blend it in visually with the flatter ends.

⑪ Use a needle file to smooth and round off the edges of both flattened ends. For each end, begin at the corner and file up and then over the top of the wire. Then flip the wire and file the other corner.

⑫ Carefully center your hole-punching pliers on one flattened end. Keep the punch away from the edges of the wire; if it is too close to an edge or the end of the wire, the pliers will break the wire rather than pierce an enclosed circle.

⑬ Firmly squeeze down the pliers to pierce a hole.

⑭ Gently twist the wire off the punch.

12

14

⑮ Turn the wire over and pierce a matching hole on the other flat end.

⑯ Use a needle file to lightly smooth any jagged edges on the surfaces where you pierced the holes.

⑰ Repeat steps 7–16 to hammer and pierce the second wire segment.

⑱ One at a time, hold each segment against the bench block and rub each side with fine steel wool until the surfaces gleam.

16

18

⑲ Polish each segment with a jewelry polishing cloth.

⑳ Working from the spool, pull several inches of 26-gauge wire through a polishing cloth to slightly straighten and polish it.

㉑ String on a bead and position it about ½ inch from the end of the 26-gauge wire.

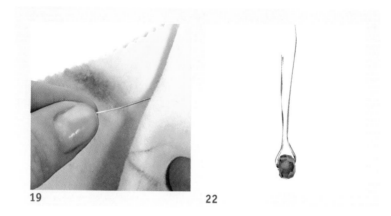

19

22

㉒ Bend the wire on both sides of the bead, and use your fingers to squeeze the ends together as if the bead were a briolette.

㉓ Use side cutters to trim the short end of the wire about 5mm from the bead.

㉔ Grasp both wires with round nose pliers, aligning the jaws with the end of the shorter wire, and bend the longer wire 90 degrees.

23

24

㉕ Reposition the pliers and use them to make a loop.

㉖ Use your fingers to slowly wrap the wire around both parallel wires between the loop and the bead, from the top down.

㉗ When you reach the point above the bead where you initially squeezed the wire together, stop wrapping and trim the wire close to the wraps.

26

27

28 Use the tips of chain nose pliers to press the wire end down gently.

29 String the wrapped bead drop you just made and a single bead onto the 26-gauge wire on the spool.

30 If necessary, run several inches of the wire through your fingers or the polishing cloth to straighten it.

31 Grasp the wire about 1 inch from its end with round nose pliers, and bend the wire 90 degrees.

31

32 Reposition the pliers to make a loop.

33 String on one of the 16-gauge wire segments and slide it into the loop.

34 Grasp the edge of the loop with chain nose or flat nose pliers (bent chain nose pliers are shown facing backward), and use your fingers or the tips of the round nose pliers to make 2 or 3 complete wraps beneath the loop.

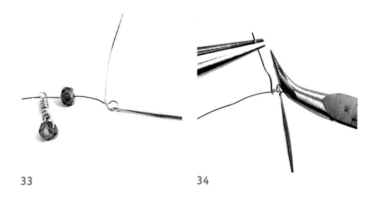

33

34

35 Trim the wire close to the wraps, and press the wire down with the tips of chain nose pliers.

36 If needed, use the tips of chain nose pliers to adjust the position of the wraps.

37 Slide the strung bead up against the wraps, and grasp the wire behind it with round nose pliers.

38 Bend the wire 90 degrees and make another loop.

36

38

39 Slide the wrapped bead drop up into the loop.

40 Make 2 or 3 complete wraps at the bottom of the loop, trim off the wire, and press down its end.

41 String the other end of the 16-gauge segment and another single bead into the 26-gauge wire still on the spool.

42 Grasp the 26-gauge wire with round nose pliers about 1 inch from the end, and bend the wire 90 degrees.

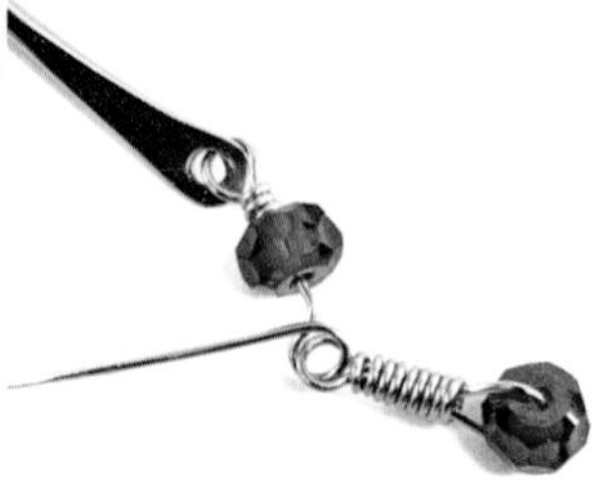

39

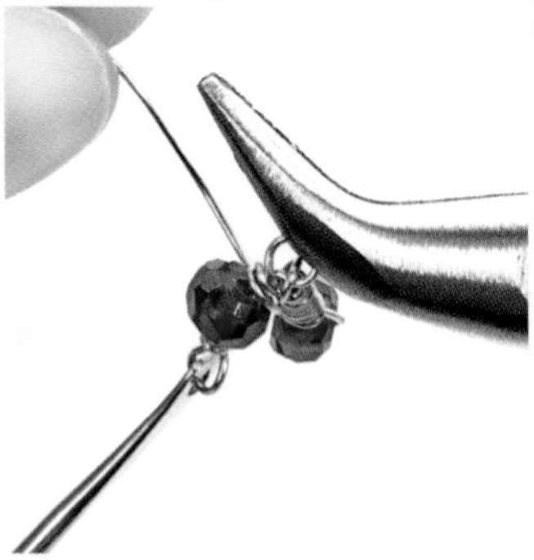

40

Wraps being made

43 Reposition the pliers to make a loop.

44 Make 2 or 3 wraps beneath the loop.

45 Trim the wire close to the wraps, and use chain nose pliers to neaten the wraps and press down the wire end.

46 Slide up the strung bead, and make another loop.

47 Slide the 16-gauge wire segment up into the loop.

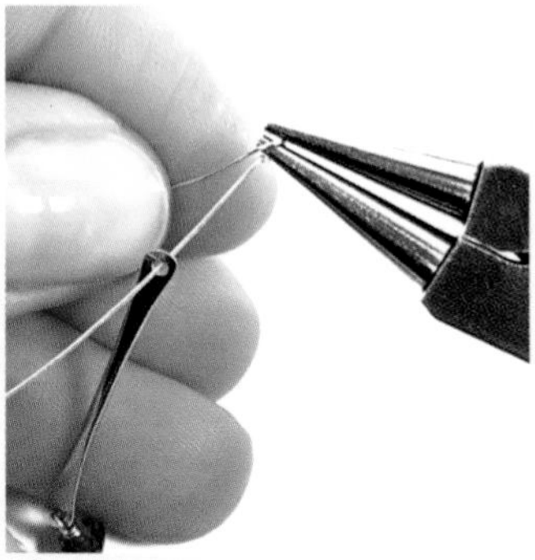

43

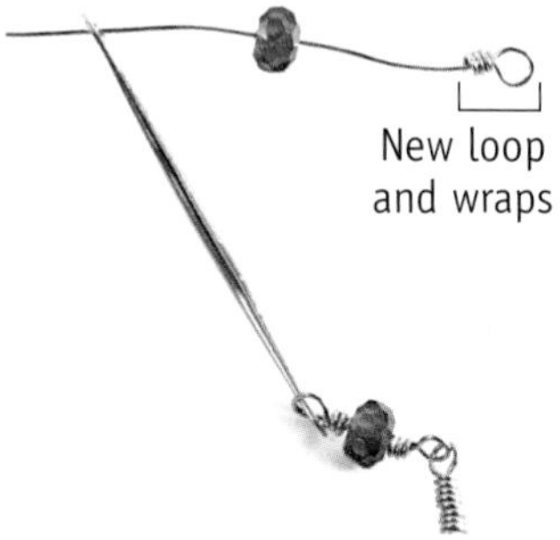

47

48 Complete the loop with wraps, and then trim, press down, and neaten the wire.

49 String another bead onto the 26-gauge wire still on the spool, and make a loop at the end just like you did in steps 42–43.

(50) Slide the empty loop from the wrapped bead that you completed in Step 48 into the loop from Step 49.

(51) Complete the loop with wraps, and then trim off, press down, and neaten the wire.

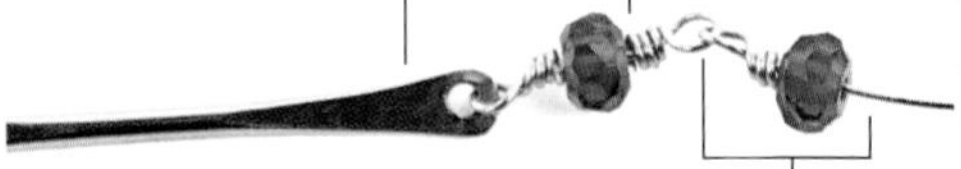

51

52. Slide up the strung bead, and complete 1 final wrapped loop.

53. Repeat steps 20–52 to assemble the beads and wire segments for the second earring.

52

54. Use 20-gauge wire to make a pair of Circular French Hooks. Pull the wire through a polishing cloth before you get started, hammer the hooks after you shape them, and then polish them again. The hooks in the example were made extra small by using a mechanical pencil as a mandrel.

55. Use chain nose or flat nose pliers to attach the beads and wire segment chains to the hooks.

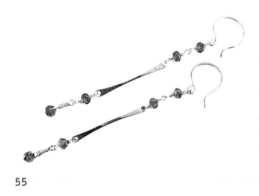

55

You can also make hammered wire segments that serve as paddle-shaped dangles. In the earrings on the right, each segment is pierced on only one end. The beads are stacked jade heishi wrapped with 24-gauge, dead-soft bronze wire.

CHAPTER 5

Embellished Hoops

You can add personality and style to hoops by decorating them with wire or beads. Use the projects in this chapter to practice some basic hoop embellishing techniques.

  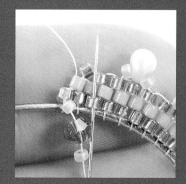

Turquoise Paisley Wraps

The glass beads in these wrapped hoops have the look of high-end turquoise gemstone. You can use this wrapping technique to adorn any hoops with the beads of your choice.

Specifications

Estimated time to complete: 30 minutes ● **Approximate size:** Just under 2 inches

TECHNIQUES

Chapter 2

- "Straighten, Cut, and File Wire"
- "Bend, Shape, and Hammer Wire"
- "Wrap Wire"

Chapter 3

- "Beading Hoops"

TOOLS AND MATERIALS

- About 11 inches of 20-gauge, round, dead-soft bronze wire
- About 28 inches of 26-gauge, round, dead-soft bronze wire
- Nylon jaw pliers (for making Beading Hoops)
- 30 Czech fire-polished 3mm glass beads in green turquoise Picasso
- Side cutters

- Medium-cut, flat needle file
- 1¼-inch (30cm) round mandrel (such as a plastic pill bottle)
- Chasing hammer
- Steel bench block
- Round nose and chain nose pliers

Make the Turquoise Paisley Wraps

1 Use 20-gauge wire and the mandrel to make a pair of round Beading Hoops. A plastic pill bottle was used as a mandrel for the hoops in the example.

2 Use a chasing hammer and steel bench block to flatten the bottom three-quarters of each hoop. Use medium force, and tap each hoop for 20–30 seconds. Doing so ensures that the dead-soft wire becomes stiff enough to hold its shape.

1

3 Use side cutters to cut a 14-inch length of 26-gauge wire.

4 Gently straighten the wire with your fingers. It does not need to be work-hardened or perfectly straight.

5 Grasp the wire about 1 inch from the end with the tips of round nose pliers, and bend it into a very small loop.

5

6 Unlatch one of the Beading Hoops and slide on the loop you just made. Position the loop so that the short end of the 26-gauge wire faces the top of the hoop.

7 Slide the loop down to about 1 inch from the top of the hoop.

7

8 Hold the short end of the 26-gauge wire against the hoop with one hand (for leverage), and use your other hand to begin wrapping the wire around the hoop frame. Start with a couple of loose wraps to anchor the wire on the hoop.

9 After making the initial loose wraps, make 3 tight wraps, taking the time to stack them one against the other. Keep the hoop unlatched so that you can bring the wire through its opening while you make wraps.

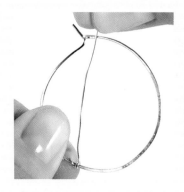

10 String a bead onto the 26-gauge wire, and position it so that its hole is parallel to the hoop frame.

11 Look down at the top of the bead, and make sure it sits diagonally on the hoop frame, as shown. (Use your fingers to adjust the 26-gauge wire as necessary.)

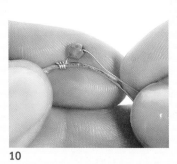

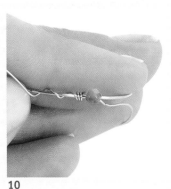

10   10

Side view   *Top view*

⑫ Use your index finger to hold the bead in place. With your other hand, wrap the wire under and around the hoop frame as close to the bead as you can. (In the example, the hoop frame was flipped over first for better leverage.)

⑬ Bring the wire down over the hoop frame again (toward the center of the hoop) to complete 1 wrap.

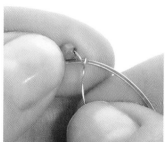

⑭ While continuing to hold the bead in place, carefully make another complete wrap (a). At the end of the wrap, position the wire so that it points away from the hoop (b).

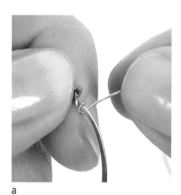
a

b

⑮ String on another bead.

⑯ Use the same technique to position the bead, and lock it into place with a second set of 2 complete wraps.

⑰ Continue stringing beads and making pairs of wraps until you have a total of 15 beads wrapped. Secure the last bead with 3 complete wraps.

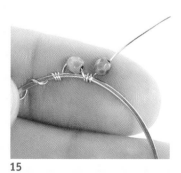
15

17

More beads being wrapped

18 Cut the 26-gauge wire close to the inside of the hoop frame.

19 Use chain nose pliers to press down the wire end.

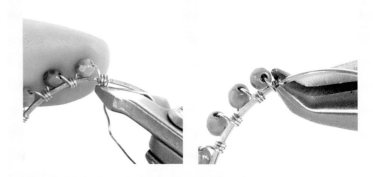

20 Go back to the first wraps that you made on the other side of the hoop, and carefully unwrap the loose wraps that you made to anchor the wire.

21 Pull the wire end down toward the center of the hoop, and trim it close to the hoop frame (just like you did in Step 18).

20

22 Repeat steps 3–21 to create a second earring. Use the first earring as a guide to help you place your initial wraps on the hoop.

Mined Gold Mosaic Hoops

These chunky hoops are filled with golden pearls and pyrite.

Specifications

Estimated time to complete: 1 hour • **Approximate size:** 3½ inches (from the tops of the hoops to the bottoms of the drops)

TECHNIQUES

Chapter 2

- "Straighten, Cut, and File Wire"
- "Bend, Shape, and Hammer Wire"

TOOLS AND MATERIALS

- About 11 inches of 18-gauge, square, dead-soft, gold-filled wire
- Nylon jaw pliers (for making Drop Hoops)
- About 54 inches of 26-gauge, round, dead-soft, gold-filled wire
- About 4 inches of 20- or 22-gauge, round, half-hard, gold-filled wire
- About 95 bronze-gold 5mm cultured pearl beads

Chapter 3

- "French Hooks"
- "Drop Hoops"

- 2 pyrite 12mm coin beads
- Side cutters
- Medium-cut, flat needle file
- 1¼-inch (30cm) round mandrel (such as a plastic pill bottle)
- Chasing hammer and steel bench block
- Round nose pliers (for making Drop Hoops)
- Flat nose and chain nose pliers

Make the Mined Gold Mosaic Earrings

① Use 18-gauge square wire and the mandrel to make a pair of Drop Hoops.

② Use the chasing hammer and bench block to work-harden each hoop. (This is important because dead-soft gold-filled wire is very pliable.) Use your fingers and/or the mandrel to readjust the shapes after hammering.

1

③ Cut a 17-inch length of 26-gauge wire and gently straighten it with your fingers. (It does not need to be perfectly straight.)

④ Use flat nose pliers to bend the last ¾ inch of 26-gauge wire into a narrow "U."

⑤ Hook the "U" around the frame of one of the hoops, next to the top loop on the frame, as shown.

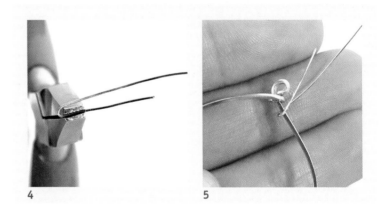

4

5

⑥ While holding the long end of the wire for leverage, wrap the short end around the frame. You can do so with your fingers, chain nose pliers, or round nose pliers.

⑦ Complete 2 more wraps with the short end of the wire. If the wire is too short to grasp well with your fingers, try using the tips of round nose pliers instead.

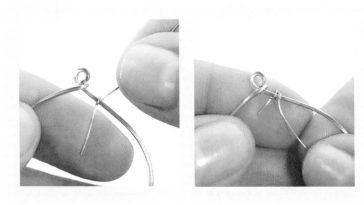

8. String 1 pearl onto the long end of the wire, and slide the pearl down against the hoop frame.

9. Bend the wire up and over the hoop frame while using your fingers to hold the pearl against the inside edge of the hoop frame.

10. Continue to hold the pearl in place with your fingers, and make 5 tight wraps around the frame. You'll need to bring the wire through the center of the hoop as you make wraps.

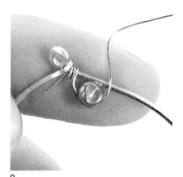
9

10

11. Turn the hoop over and use side cutters to trim off the short wire tail close to the frame.

12. Use the tips of chain nose pliers to press the wire end down against the frame.

13. String 4 pearls and bring the wire to the opposite side of the hoop frame, as shown. Bend the wire so that the line of 4 pearls arcs around the first pearl that you wrapped.

14. Hold the 4 pearls in place, and make 5 tight wraps around the hoop frame. Use your index finger to push each wrap into place before tightening it down.

⑮ Use chain nose pliers to gently squeeze the wraps together and neaten them up.

⑯ String on 6 pearls, bring the wire back to the other side of the hoop, and complete 5 more tight wraps. If the wire starts to kink, use your fingers to gently straighten it.

⑰ String on 8 pearls, bring the wire back to the other side of the hoop, and complete 5 more wraps. (Continue to use the chain nose pliers to neaten your wraps as needed.)

⑱ String on 7 pearls, and this time bring the wire diagonally down across the frame.

17

⑲ Make 5 tight wraps around the hoop frame directly below the last pearl that you strung in Step 18.

⑳ String on 6 pearls, bring the wire to the opposite side of the frame below the 7 pearls from Step 18, and make 5 wraps below the last pearl that you strung.

21 String on 5 pearls, and bring the wire to the other side.

22 Make 5 more tight wraps around the frame. Because space is limited, these wraps can be more challenging than the previous ones. Gently feed the wire through from the front of the hoop frame (a), and then turn the frame over and pull it tight from the back (b).

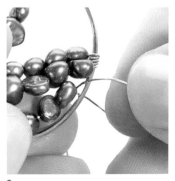
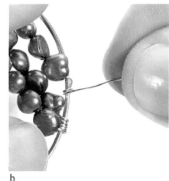

a

b

23 Trim off the wire close to the frame, and press it down with chain nose pliers.

24 Cut a new length of about 6 inches of 26-gauge wire.

25 Use chain nose pliers to bend the last ¾ inch into a narrow "U," and hook it around the hoop frame in the upper portion of the frame that remains without beads.

23

26 Using the short end of the wire for leverage, create 5 tight wraps, moving downward along the frame.

27 String on 4 or 5 pearls, bring the wire down to the bottom of the empty space, and make 5 wraps there, moving upward along the frame. Because space is limited, you may need to use chain nose or flat nose pliers (shown) to pull each wrap tight.

Frame rotated 45° to the left

28 String a final set of 2 or 3 pearls, bring the wire across the frame below the previous 4 pearls, and make another set of 5 wraps upward along the frame. Use chain nose or flat nose pliers to pull each wrap tight.

29 Trim off the wire tails close to the hoop frame, and press them down against the frame with chain nose pliers.

28

30 Cut a new 4-inch length of 26-gauge wire, and use flat nose pliers to create a narrow "U" about ¾ inch from one end.

31 Hook the "U" over the hoop frame just above the second set of wraps from the bottom on the left side, as shown.

31

32 Use chain nose pliers to wrap the short end of the wire around the frame, through the center of the hoop.

33 Continue to use chain nose pliers (rather than your fingers) to wrap the short end of the wire around the frame until you have 3 or 4 wraps. Finish with the wire resting across the front of the frame.

32

34) String on 1 pearl, 1 pyrite bead, and 4 more pearls.

35) Bring the wire up across the front of the hoop so that it crosses just to the left of the loop at the top of the frame.

36) Use chain nose pliers to carefully make 3 or 4 tight wraps around the frame. This space is very tight, so take your time.

37) Trim both remaining wire ends close to the frame, and press them down with chain nose pliers.

36

38) Repeat steps 3–37 to create a second, matching hoop.

39) Use 22-gauge wire to make a pair of Bail-Maker French Hooks or Circular French Hooks.

40) Use chain nose or flat nose pliers to open the bottom loop on each ear wire, and attach it to the top loop on a hoop.

FAQ

What should I do if my wrapping wire breaks?

Recall from Chapter 2 that wire becomes more brittle the more you bend it. Bend wire only as much as necessary, even when you make wraps. If at any point your wire breaks, use side cutters to trim off the mangled portion, and end the wire by wrapping it around the frame and pressing it down with chain nose pliers. Begin a new length of wire by wrapping it several times on top of (or next to) the wraps you made to finish off the old wire. Continue your project with the new wire.

A broken wrapping wire

Lace Edge Loops

With this wrapping technique, you make wire wraps that are absent of beads. You can wear the earrings with the wraps alone ("Simple Lace Edge Loops"), or add ruffles of decorative beadwork ("Beaded Lace Edge Hoops").

Specifications

Estimated time to complete: 30 minutes for simple loops; 2 hours for beaded loops ● **Approximate size:** 1½ inches long x 1¼ inches wide for simple loops; 1¾ inches long x 1¼ inches wide for beaded loops

TECHNIQUES

SIMPLE LACE EDGE LOOPS

The following techniques are used to make earrings without beads:

Chapter 2

- "Straighten, Cut, and File Wire"
- "Bend Wire"
- "Shape Wire"

Chapter 3

- "Beading Hoops"

BEADED LACE EDGE LOOPS

The following techniques are used to add beads to your earrings:

Chapter 2

- "Pulling and Cutting Beading Thread"
- "Waxing or Conditioning Nylon Thread"
- "Threading a Beading Needle"
- "Positioning the Needle"
- "Picking Up Beads"
- "How to Read a Bead Key"
- "Stitching Beads"

TOOLS AND MATERIALS

SIMPLE LACE EDGE LOOPS

Use the following tools and materials to make earrings without beads:

- About 10 inches of 22-gauge, half-hard, round, antiqued-bronze wire
- Nylon jaw pliers (for making Beading Hoops)
- 24 inches of Artistic 24-gauge colored copper wire in gunmetal
- Chasing hammer and steel bench block
- Side cutters
- Round nose and chain nose pliers
- 1¼-inch (30mm) round mandrel
- Medium-cut, flat needle file
- Fine-tip permanent marker
- Brass gauge

BEADED LACE EDGE LOOPS

Use the following tools and materials to add beads to your earrings:

- 32 size 15/0 round Miyuki seed beads in opaque luster rainbow medium blue (**A**)*
- 32 Toho magatama 3mm beads in gold-lined rainbow aqua (**B**)
- 64 size 15/0 round Miyuki seed beads in opaque luster baby blue (**C**)*
- 32 Toho magatama 3mm beads in gold luster green tea (**D**)
- 16 Toho magatama 3mm beads in gold-lined rainbow light jonquil (**E**)
- Beading scissors
- C-Lon size D beading thread in light blue
- Thread conditioner
- 2 size 12 beading needles
- Optional: Magnifier (to help you see your beadwork)

*Manufacturers change their seed bead colors over time. If you can't find the exact colors used in the example, you can use any medium light blue for **A** and any pale light blue for **C**.

Make the Simple Lace Edge Loops

① Make 2 Beading Hoops using 22-gauge wire and the mandrel. Be sure to tap the hoops lightly with a chasing hammer on a bench block to harden their temper.

② Cut a 12-inch length of 24-gauge wire from the spool, and use your fingers to gently straighten it.

③ Use the tips of round nose pliers to make a tiny loop about 1 inch from one end of the 24-gauge wire.

④ Unlatch one of the Beading Hoops, and slide on the tiny loop of 24-gauge wire. Position the loop so that the short tail of wire faces the top of the hoop frame and is about 1⅛ inches down.

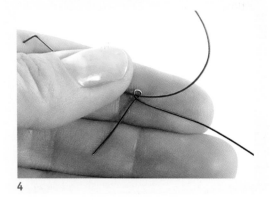

4

⑤ Using the short wire tail for leverage, make 2 or 3 loose wraps around the hoop frame to anchor the 24-gauge wire. Then make 3 wraps stacked closely side by side. (If they don't line up perfectly, you can use chain nose pliers to adjust them.)

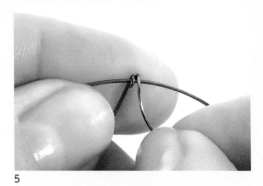

5

Some initial loose wraps

⑥ Use a fine-tip permanent marker to mark your round nose pliers at the point where their jaws are 2mm in diameter. (The mark will wear off over time.)

⑦ With the 24-gauge wire running up alongside the hoop frame, grasp the hoop frame against the last wrap with your round nose pliers. Align the mark on the pliers with the hoop frame.

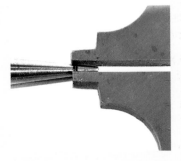

Brass gauge measuring the pliers' diameter

8 Use your other hand to bring the 24-gauge wire over the round nose pliers, toward the center of the hoop.

9 Wrap the wire all the way around the hoop frame against the jaws of the pliers. Work slowly and deliberately to position the wrap. Be careful not to pull so tightly that you bend the hoop frame.

10 Remove the pliers from the frame.

11 Repeat steps 7–10 seven more times along the hoop frame.

12 Make 3 tightly stacked wraps around the hoop frame to complete the wirework.

NOTE: If any spaces form between the wraps, you can use flat nose pliers to gently squeeze them together.

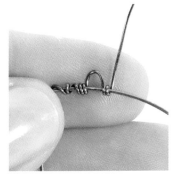

10

12

13 Use side cutters to trim the 24-gauge wire close to the last 3 wraps, and press the wire down against the hoop frame with chain nose pliers.

14 Return to the beginning of the 24-gauge wire, and unwrap the initial loose wraps from Step 5.

15 Trim and press down the wire, just like you did in Step 13.

16 Repeat steps 2–15 to complete a second, matching earring.

Make the Beaded Lace Edge Loops

1. Make a pair of Simple Lace Edge Loops.

2. Prepare a 20-inch length of size D beading thread, and thread a size 12 beading needle onto each end.

3. Pass a needle up through the first lace loop on one of the earrings.

4. Pick up the other needle and center the earring on the thread.

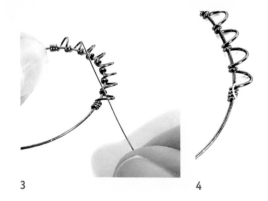

3

4

5. Use a needle to pick up and string the following beads (see the materials list on page XXX for the bead key): 1A, 1B, 1C, 1D, 1C, 1E.

6. Use the second needle to pick up and string the following beads: 1A, 1B, 1C, 1D, 1C.

7. Use your fingers to slide the beads on both halves of the thread down toward the earring.

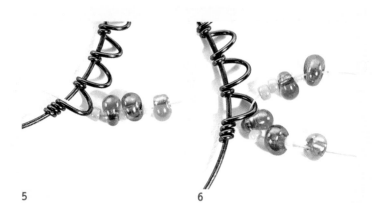

5

6

8. Tie a square knot with the 2 thread ends, and cinch the knot down against the beads to create a small beaded circle. (Until you get comfortable making square knots with beading thread, you may find it helpful to remove both needles before making the knot.)

9. Tie a second square knot directly on top of the first.

10. If you removed the needles in Step 8, thread each one back onto its respective thread end.

⑪ Pick up the earring, and hold the beaded circle between your fingers. (The beadwork is lying flat in the photo on the right to better show the thread path.)

⑫ Use one needle to pass through all the beads in the circle again, starting with the adjacent magatama bead. Pull the square knots into that bead's hole. Go through 1 or 2 beads at a time, stopping along the way to pull the thread taut. Be careful not to skip beads. Position the needle against the inside of each bead hole to avoid splitting the existing thread.

11

⑬ Switch to the other needle and, going in the opposite direction, pass it through at least 3 or 4 beads in the circle.

⑭ Pull both threads taut, and use beading scissors to trim them very close to the beads. Be careful not to cut the thread that holds the circle together.

⑮ Repeat steps 2–14 for the remaining 7 wire lace loops on this earring and all 8 lace loops on the other earring.

Your fringy, beaded loop earrings are now complete.

Stacked Bead Drop Hoops

These colorful earrings are made by stitching beads within modified drop hoops. Once you understand the technique, you can experiment with different colors and vary the number of beads.

Specifications

Estimated time to complete: 45 minutes–1 hour • **Approximate size:** 1¾ inches from the tops of the hooks to the bottoms of the hoops x ⅝ inch wide

TECHNIQUES

The following techniques are used to make the Drop Hoops and ear wires:

Chapter 2

- "Straighten, Cut, and File Wire"
- "Bend, Shape, and Hammer Wire"
- Optional: "Create a Patina with Liver of Sulfur"
- "Open and Close Jump Rings"

The following techniques are used to stitch the beads:

- "Pulling and Cutting Beading Thread"
- "Threading a Beading Needle"
- "Positioning the Needle"
- "Picking Up Beads"
- "Stitching Beads"
- "Weaving-In"
- "Making Half Hitch Knots"
- "Using a Thread Burner"
- "How to Read a Bead Key"
- "Common Beadwork Terms"

Chapter 3

- "Beading Hoops"
- "Bail-Maker French Hooks"

TOOLS AND MATERIALS

The following tools and materials are used to make and connect the Drop Hoops and ear wires:

- About 14 inches of 18-gauge, dead-soft, round wire in the metal of your choice
- About 4 inches of matching 20-gauge wire
- Nylon jaw pliers
- Medium-cut, flat needle file
- Two 18-gauge jump rings with an outside diameter of about 5.5mm–6mm
- Round nose pliers
- 1¼-inch (30cm) round mandrel
- Graduated ring mandrel
- Chasing hammer and steel bench block

The following tools and materials are used to create the beadwork:

- 4-pound FireLine beading thread in crystal
- Hobby knife or children's craft scissors (for cutting FireLine)
- Size 12 beading needle
- Size 11/0 round seed beads in the color of your choice (**A**)
- Size 15/0 round seed beads in the color of your choice (**B**)
- Thread burner
- Optional: Toothpick and clear nail polish
- Optional: Liver of sulfur, latex gloves, water, paper towels, and fine steel wool (for creating a patina)

The earrings in the example are made with dead-soft sterling silver wire. The size 11/0 seed beads are Miyuki opaque matte moss green, and the size 15/0 seed beads are Miyuki metallic matte turquoise.

Make the Stacked Bead Drop Hoops

1 Use 18-gauge wire and the 1¼-inch mandrel to perform steps 1–11 of "Beading Hoops" in Chapter 3.

2 Use the tips of round nose pliers to bend each end of each wire backward into a small loop, as shown.

3 Stack the 2 loops on each wire and slide them into an open jump ring. Close the jump ring to hold the loops together.

2   3

4 Slide each hoop, one at a time, onto a graduated ring mandrel until it fits snugly, and press the sides of the hoop down over the mandrel to make its shape rounder. Align the top of each hoop with the groove in the ring mandrel. Remove each hoop after shaping it.

TIP

Use your graduated mandrel as needed

You can return the hoop to the graduated mandrel to adjust the hoop's shape at any time before you begin the beadwork. Doing so can be especially helpful after hammering (see Step 5), which always has the potential to deform your wire shapes slightly.

5 Use a chasing hammer and bench block to flatten the curve of each loop. (Remember to position the loops and jump ring over the edge of the bench block so that the hoop lies flat.)

NOTE: If you want to give your earrings a patina, apply it now.

6 Cut an arm's-span length of FireLine, and thread the needle. Fold over a thread tail about 6 inches long.

7 Pick up 1A with the needle.

8 Slide the 1A down to about 8–10 inches from the end of the thread, and position it beneath the hoop frame. In the photo, the thread tail stretches up toward the right, and the needle end of the thread is trailing down toward the left.

9 While using your fingers to hold the 1A in position (not shown), bring the needle beneath the hoop to the front side of the hoop, and pass the needle up through the 1A.

10 Hold the 1A against the frame, and pull the thread taut. Notice that the bead hole is perpendicular to the frame.

11 Tie a square knot with the 2 threads against the bead.

5

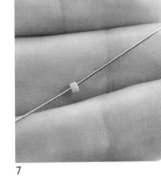

7

After hammering

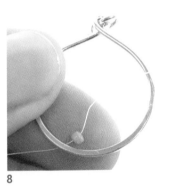

8

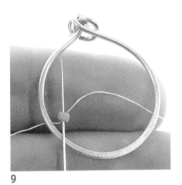

9

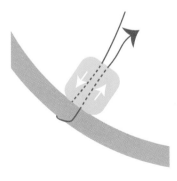

The thread path

The bead in place and the thread pulled taut

⓬ Slide the bead up on the hoop frame to the place you want to begin beading.

⓭ Position the needle end of the thread so that it runs behind the hoop frame (rather than in front of it).

⓮ Pick up another 1A and slide it down against the hoop frame, next to the first 1A.

⓯ Bring the needle under the frame to the front side (allowing the second 1A to flip upside down on the frame) and pass up through the second 1A.

15

⓰ Pass the needle through the hoop to the back of the frame (not shown).

⓱ Hold the second 1A in place against the frame, and pull the thread taut. You now have a second bead stitched in place.

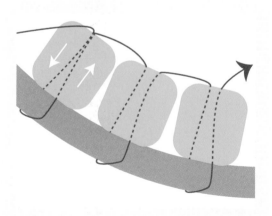

17

⓲ Continue this process to stitch the entire first row of beads. You can make this row any length, as long as it contains a total number of beads divisible by 3. (This keeps the pattern in the second row even.) In the example, 18 beads are stitched for the first row.

NOTE: If at any time the short thread tail gets in the way of your working thread, take a moment to gently pull the tail free.

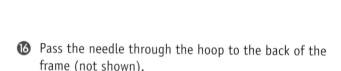

19 To begin the second row of beads, pick up 2B and slide them down against the first row.

20 Stitching from the back to the front of the frame, pass the needle beneath the bridge of thread that runs between the second from last and third from last beads in the first row.

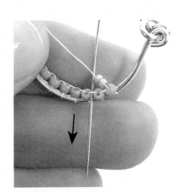

21 While using your fingers to hold the second B in place (not shown), pass up through the hole in that bead—in front of the bridge of thread—and pull your thread taut.

22 Pass down through the first B and the last bead in the first row and pull the thread taut.

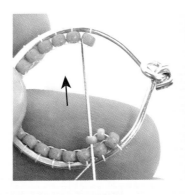
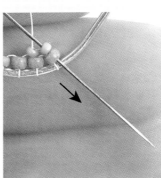

FAQ

How can I keep a bead from sliding up the thread before a stitch is complete?

With brick stitch, it's important to hold each bead in place against the beadwork while you stitch. After picking up a bead and sliding it down against the bridge of thread, use the fingers of your non-dominant hand to hold the thread down taut while you use your other hand to pass the needle back up into the bead (left). Then let go of the thread with your non-dominant hand, and grab onto the bead itself. Continue holding the bead while using your other hand to pull the thread taut (right).

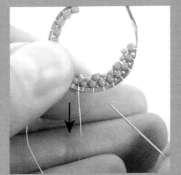

㉓ Pass up through the second from last bead in the first row and the second B in the second row, and pull the thread taut. (This "weaving through" procedure is part of basic brick stitch; it helps lock the first 2 beads in a row in place.)

㉔ Pass the needle through the hoop to the back of the frame and pick up 1A.

The first 2 beads in the second row stitched on

㉕ With the 1A still on the needle, pass the needle down beneath the bridge of thread running between the next 2 beads on the frame.

㉖ Pull the thread gently taut, and allow the 1A to slide against the bridge of thread.

㉗ Pass back up through the 1A—in front of the bridge of thread—and pull your thread taut.

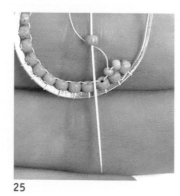
25

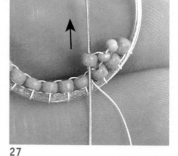
27

㉘ Continue the following process to stitch 1 bead at a time: Pick up a bead from behind the frame, pass beneath the next bridge of thread, and pass back up through the bead. Use this general sequence to bead the entire row: 1B, 1B, 1A, 1B, 1B, 1A, 1B, 1B, 1A, 1B, 1B, 1A, 1B, 1B, and so on. This row should have 1 bead fewer than the first row.

29 Begin to weave-in the thread by passing down diagonally through 2 beads, as shown. Pull the thread taut.

30 Turn the hoop over, and pass up through 2 beads diagonally on the other side. Pull the thread taut again.

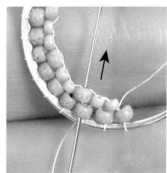

31 Tie a half hitch knot around the next bridge of thread that runs between 2 beads.

32 Changing direction, pass down through the next single bead, and pull the thread taut once again.

32

33 Wrap the thread around your fingers to hold its tension, as shown, and use a thread burner in your other hand to cut the thread close to the beadwork.

34 Thread the needle onto the thread tail that you left hanging down when you began stitching the beads.

33

35 Use the same technique to weave-in and end the thread tail. You may need to pass through just 1 bead at a time as the thread begins to fill the bead holes.

36 Optionally, use a toothpick to apply a tiny drop of clear nail polish to the bottom of the first bead in the second row, and press it down against the first row until it remains tacked down. (This bead is prone to tipping forward toward the center of the hoop.)

36

37 Repeat steps 6–36 to create a second beaded hoop.

38 Use 20-gauge wire to make a pair of French hooks, and use chain nose and/or flat nose pliers to attach them to the jump rings on your completed hoops. The French hooks in the example are Bail-Maker French Hooks (see Chapter 3).

TIP

You can also stitch beads inside metal rings

Try using the same technique to stitch beads on the inside of ready-made pendant findings like the 30mm gold-plated rings shown here. Each hoop is made with 39 size 11/0 galvanized gold seed beads in the first round, and a combination of size 11/0 gold and size 15/0 metallic iris seed beads in the second round. As you complete each round, pass down through the first bead and up through the last bead again to stitch those beads together. With this approach, you can forgo the reinforcing stitches that occur at the beginning of each round in the Stacked Bead Drop Hoops.

Pearl Flamingo Hoops

These frilly, bead-woven hoops take brick stitch to the next level. You make them by stitching beads on the outside of each hoop frame.

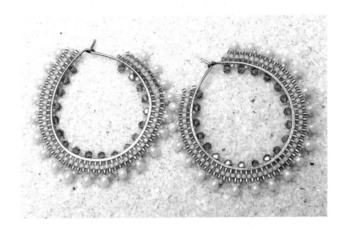

Estimated time to complete: 1½ hours ● **Approximate size:** 1¼ inches long and 2 inches wide

TECHNIQUES

Chapter 2

- "Straighten, Cut, and File Wire"
- "Bend, Shape, and Hammer Wire"
- "Pulling and Cutting Beading Thread"
- "Threading a Beading Needle"
- "Positioning the Needle"

- "Picking Up Beads"
- "Stitching Beads"
- "Making Half Hitch Knots"
- "Using a Thread Burner"
- "How to Read a Bead Key"
- "Common Beadwork Terms"

TOOLS AND MATERIALS

- About 12 inches of 20-gauge, half-hard, sterling silver wire
- 1¼-inch (30mm) round mandrel
- Side cutters
- Nylon jaw pliers and medium-cut, flat needle file (for making Beading Hoops)
- Chasing hammer and steel bench block
- About 130 size 11/0 Delica cylinder beads in each of 4 colors: sparkling lined sand dune mix (**A**),

opaque salmon (**B**), sparkling green lined topaz (**C**), silver-lined matte rainbow light gold (**D**)

- About 40 Miyuki 3.4mm drop beads in opaque luster beige (**E**)
- About 38 Chinese crystal 4mm bicones in topaz (**F**)
- Size 12 beading needle
- 4-pound FireLine beading thread in crystal
- Hobby knife or children's craft scissors
- Thread burner

Make the Pearl Flamingo Hoops

① Use 20-gauge wire and the mandrel to create a pair of Beading Hoops.

② Hammer and slightly flatten the curves of the hoops with a chasing hammer and bench block.

③ If you'd like, oxidize the hoops with liver of sulfur. (The hoops in the example were lightly oxidized and brushed with steel wool.)

④ Cut a 9-foot length of FireLine, and thread the needle.

⑤ Pick up 1A and slide it down to about 8–10 inches from the end of the thread.

⑥ Use your fingers to position the 1A against the outside of the hoop frame, with the hole parallel to the frame wire. Position the thread so that it runs behind the hoop frame.

⑦ Pass the needle up through the center of the frame, and then up through the 1A.

⑧ While still holding the 1A in place with your fingers, pull the thread gently taut. Because you are working with very long thread, you need to pull it slowly to avoid tangling.

⑨ Tie a square knot with both ends of thread at the end of the 1A.

⑩ Pick another 1A, and slide it down to the hoop frame.

⑪ Turn this bead upside down so that the thread exits toward the hoop frame and falls behind the hoop frame.

⑫ Pass the needle up through the center of the frame, and then up through the second 1A.

3

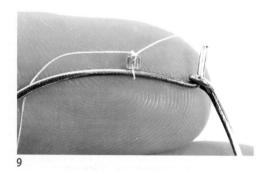

9

12

13 Slowly pull the thread taut.

NOTE: If at any time the short thread tail gets in the way of your working thread, take a moment to gently pull it free before completing the stitch.

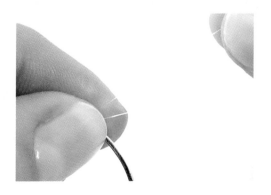

14 Repeat steps 10–13 to stitch beads all the way around the bead frame, leaving an unbeaded space of about ¼ inch at the top of the hoop, just behind the place where the wire is bent upward 90 degrees. This is the space that passes through your ear. If the thread begins to twist up on itself, stop and carefully straighten it to avoid knots and tangles.

15 To begin the second row, pick up 2B and pass the needle toward you beneath the bridge of thread that runs between the second and third from last beads in the first row.

16 Pull the thread gently taut.

17 Hold the second B between your fingers and pass the needle back up through that bead, in front of the bridge of thread. Pull your thread taut again to complete the stitch.

15

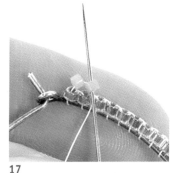

17

18 Weave through the beads to lock the first 2 beads in place, using the thread path shown on the right. This is the same thread path used in steps 22–23 of Stacked Bead Hoop Drops (pages 115–116).

19 To begin the next stitch, pick up 1B and pass the needle toward you beneath the very next bridge of thread in the first row. Allow the 1B to come to rest against that thread.

20 Pass the needle back up through the 1B, in front of the bridge of thread, to complete the stitch.

21 Repeat steps 19–20 to stitch B beads until you have covered approximately half of the first row of beads.

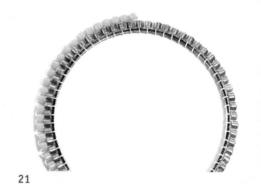

21

22 In order for the beadwork to lie relatively flat, the second row needs to be longer than the first row. You achieve this by making an *increase*. Pick up the next 1B and pass the needle toward you beneath the *same* bridge of thread that you passed under to stitch the previous 1B (a). Pass back up through the 1B, as usual, to complete the increase (b).

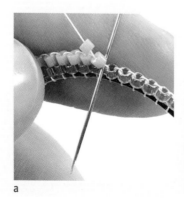

a

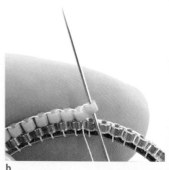

b

23 Stitch the next 1B by passing beneath the next bridge of thread.

24 Continue stitching single B beads without increases until you reach the beginning of the first row of beads.

25 Stitch 2C to begin the third row, locking these 2 beads in place as usual when beginning a row of brick stitch (see Step 18).

25

26 Stitch the entire row of C beads, making an increase at each of the 3 approximate locations marked by asterisks as shown at right.

NOTE: If your frame dimensions differ from those in the example, you may need slightly fewer or more increases in order to keep your beadwork flat. Use your best judgment. If your beadwork begins to cup, stop and make an additional increase.

27 The next row is a round of beaded picot edging. Begin by picking up 1D, 1E, 1D and sliding them down against the beadwork.

28 Pass the needle down through the third from last bead in the third row, and pull the thread gently taut.

29 Pass up through the next bead in the third row, and pull the thread taut again.

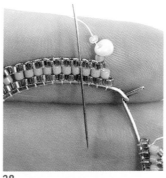

28

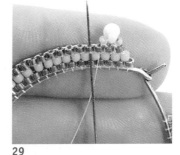

29

30 Pick up another set of 1D, 1E, 1D; skip a bead in the third row; and pass down into the next bead.

31 Pull the thread taut, and pass up through the next bead in the third row.

32 Continue this process to stitch picots of 3 beads each all the way around the hoop frame, until there are too few beads remaining in the third row to fit any more picots.

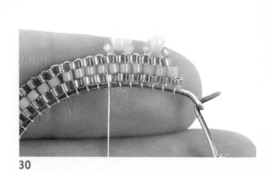

30

33 Weave down through the beadwork until your thread exits the last bead in the first row. Pass through 1 bead at a time, using a path that keeps the thread hidden (see the example thread path at right).

34 To begin the inside embellishment, pick up 1D, 1F, 1D, and pass up through the third from last bead in the first row.

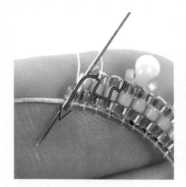

35 Pull the thread taut, and then reverse direction by passing down through the very next bead in the first row.

36 Pull the thread taut again, and pick up another set of 1D, 1F, 1D.

37 Skip a bead in the first row, and pass up through the following bead in that row.

38 Continue this process to stitch sets of 3 beads along the entire hoop frame until there are too few beads remaining in the first row to fit in another set.

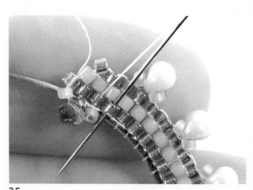

35

39 Optional: If 1 or 2 beads are left unembellished in the first row, pick up 1D or 2D and stitch them over those beads (that is, stitch 1 or 2 beads rather than the full set of 3).

40 Pass up into the second row of beadwork, and tie a half hitch knot over the existing thread to preserve the working thread's tension.

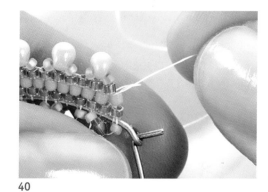

40

41 Weave through the beadwork and the last (or second to last) set of 3 embellishment beads. Weave through all the embellishment beads again to reinforce them. The correct path is shown at right.

42 When you reach the other side of the hoop, weave-in the thread with 2 or 3 half hitch knots, and cut it close to the beadwork with a thread burner.

43 Thread the needle on the original thread tail, weave-in that tail, and end that thread.

41

44 Make a second earring to complete your pair. When you reach Step 33, be sure to bring your needle out on what will be the front side of the hoop when you wear your earrings; the completed earrings should be mirror images of one another.

CHAPTER 6

Boho Inspirations

Bohemian designs are casual and earthy. The earrings in this chapter feature feathers, leather, chains, and a variety of beads.

Pins and Leather Earrings

Ready-made head pins, leather cord, and beads come together in these quick and casual earrings.

Specifications

Estimated time to complete: 30 minutes • **Approximate length:** 2 inches

TECHNIQUES
Chapter 2

- "Cut Wire"
- "File Wire"
- "Bend, Shape, and Hammer Wire"

- "Make Simple Connector Loops"
- "Open and Close Simple Connector Loops"
- "Wrap Wire Over Wire"

TOOLS AND MATERIALS

- 10 black or gunmetal finish 2-inch, 21-gauge, ball-end head pins
- 4 inches of black Greek leather 2mm round cord
- 20 stabilized blue turquoise 3mm–5mm nugget beads
- Side cutters

- Bail-making pliers
- Round nose and chain nose pliers
- Chasing hammer and steel bench block
- Medium-cut, flat needle file
- Ruler (for measuring leather)

Make the Pins and Leather Earrings

❶ Grasp a head pin next to its ball end with round nose pliers, and roll that end into a connector loop.

❷ Grasp the center of the head pin with bail-making pliers, and bend the pin into a "U" around the larger of the 2 barrels.

❸ Use the bail-making pliers to slightly bend back the straight end of the pin.

❹ Using a chasing hammer and steel bench block, hammer the rounded "U" portion of the pin to slightly flatten and stiffen it.

❺ Pinch the new ear wire with your fingers and thumb to bring the 2 sides closer together.

❻ Use a needle file to debur the end of the ear wire.

3

5

❼ Use side cutters to flush-cut a 2-inch segment of leather cord.

❽ Hold the ball end of a head pin perpendicular to the leather ¼ inch from one end of the leather.

❾ Wrap the pin around the leather as if you were wrapping wire around another wire. It is important to make the wrap very tight.

❿ Keep wrapping until you reach the end of the leather cord.

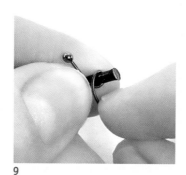

9

10

⑪ Use round nose pliers to make a "U"-shaped loop with the head pin, rolling the loop toward the cut edge of the cord.

⑫ Perform steps 8–11 on the other end of the cord to make a matching coil and loop there.

⑬ Use chain nose pliers to connect one loop to the other.

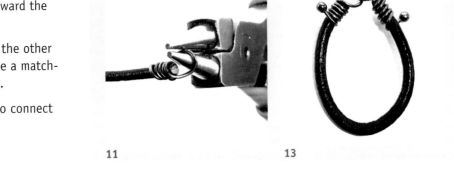

11

13

⑭ String 6 turquoise beads onto a new head pin.

⑮ Use side cutters to trim the head pin ¼ inch from the last turquoise bead.

⑯ Use round nose pliers to roll the end of the pin into a small connector loop.

⑰ Connect that loop to one of the loops on the leather cord.

16

17

⑱ String 4 beads onto another head pin, trim the pin, and make a connector loop.

⑲ Attach the second beaded pin to the empty loop on the leather cord.

⑳ Attach the ear wire that you made in Step 6 to the loop on the cord that contains the longer of the 2 beaded pins.

㉑ Repeat steps 1–20 to make a matching earring for your pair.

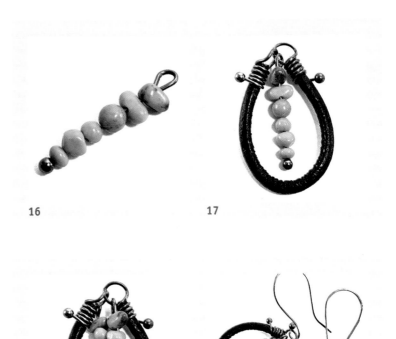

19

21

These enameled filigree earrings are reminiscent of coral and sand.

Specifications

Estimated time to complete: 35 minutes • **Approximate length:** 3 inches

TECHNIQUES

Chapter 2

- "Straighten, Cut, and File Wire"
- "Bend, Shape, and Hammer Wire"
- "Make Simple Connector Loops"
- "Open and Close Simple Connector Loops"

TOOLS AND MATERIALS

- 2 brown enameled filigree "kaleidoscope" laser stampings (try www.rings-things.com)
- 10 peach moonstone 4mm–5mm gem-faceted rondelle beads (try www.beadaholique.com)
- 6 Vintaj Natural Brass 5mm jump rings
- 12 inches of 26-gauge, round, dead-soft bronze wire
- 4 inches of 20-gauge, round, dead-soft bronze wire
- 24 inches of 24-gauge, round, dead-soft bronze wire

- "Open and Close Jump Rings"
- "Wrap Wire Over Wire"
- "Wire Wrap Regular Beads"

Chapter 3

- "Circular French Hooks"

- Medium-cut, flat needle file
- Chasing hammer and steel bench block
- Side cutters
- Round nose and chain nose pliers
- Ruler (for measuring wire)
- Flat nose pliers or second pair of chain nose pliers
- Flat nylon jaw pliers and mandrel

Make the Beach Flower Earrings

1 Use your fingers to gently straighten 6 inches of 26-gauge wire still on the spool.

2 Use side cutters to cut off that 6 inches of wire.

3 String on a peach moonstone bead, and center it on the wire.

4 Bend up both sides of the wire so that the bead is in the bottom of a wire "U."

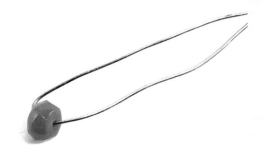

4

5 Pass both ends of the wire through 2 opposing pierced petals that surround the hole at the center of one of the filigrees.

6 Hold the bead down against the front of the filigree, and fold both wires down toward each other on the back.

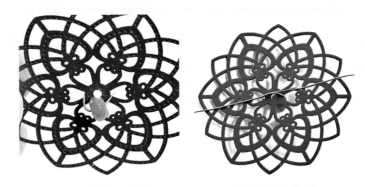

7 Pass one end of the wire back through the filigree in the same petal that contains the other end of the wire.

8 While holding the bead in position with your finger, slowly wrap the wire around one side of the petal (with the back of the filigree facing you) 3 times. Use your fingers to straighten out any sharp bends in the wire as you make the wraps to keep the wire from kinking.

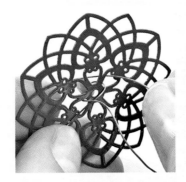

⑨ Use side cutters to cut the wire close to the wraps on the back of the filigree.

⑩ Use chain nose pliers to press down the end of the trimmed wire.

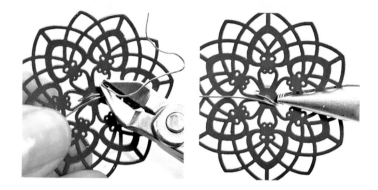

⑪ Pass the other wire end up through the filigree the same way you did with the first end of the wire.

⑫ Make 3 wraps, press down the wire end, and trim the wire close to the wraps on the back of the filigree.

⑬ Use your fingers to gently straighten several inches of 24-gauge wire still on the spool.

⑭ String on 2 moonstone beads. (If either of the beads does not fit on the wire, try a different bead; gemstone bead hole sizes vary.)

⑮ Lay the end of the wire on your bench block, and use a chasing hammer to flatten its end.

⑯ Slide the 2 beads down firmly on the wire until they meet the hammered end and can't slide any farther.

16

17. Use round nose pliers to make a wrapped loop on the unhammered end of the wire.

18. Use side cutters to trim the wire close to the wraps, and chain nose pliers to press down the wire end. Do so gently to avoid pushing the beads farther down the wire.

19. Use side cutters to trim the hammered end of the wire about ⅛ inch from the beads.

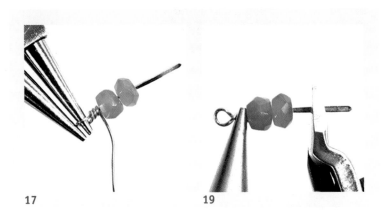

17

19

20. Use a needle file to smooth and round the corners of the cut that you just made.

21. Use a jump ring to attach the drop that you just made to the pierced hole in the filigree that will be at the bottom center of the earring, as shown.

22. Use the technique from steps 13–20 to make 2 more beaded drops, but string on only 1 bead each.

23. Use jump rings to attach those drops to the filigree in the locations shown.

24. Repeat steps 1–23 to make a second beaded filigree.

25. Use the 20-gauge wire to make a pair of Circular French Hooks.

26. Attach the ear wires to the tops of the filigrees, with the unlooped ends of the ear wires pointing toward the backs of the filigrees, to complete the pair.

26

In this design, soft peacock and rooster feathers create a striking backdrop for pearl bead drops and chains.

Specifications

Estimated time to complete: 35 minutes ● **Approximate length:** 4 inches

TECHNIQUES

Chapter 2

- "Straighten Wire"
- "Cut Wire"
- "Open and Close Simple Connector Loops"
- "Open and Close Jump Rings"

- "Wire Wrap Regular Beads"
- "Cut Closed-Link Chain"
- "Picking Up Beads"

Chapter 3

- "Circular French Hooks"

TOOLS AND MATERIALS

- 2 long peacock saddle plumage feathers (look for feathers at www.moonlightfeather.com)

- 2 slightly shorter peacock saddle plumage feathers

- 2 tan, grizzly rooster fluff feathers

- White craft glue and toothpicks

- 2 gold-plated, 6.5mm x 5mm fold-over cord ends

- 2 gold-plated or brass, 4.5mm, 20-gauge jump rings

- 7 inches of gold-plated 5mm x 3.5mm cable chain

- 16 gold-plated, 1½-inch, 21-gauge head pins

- About 4 inches of 20-gauge, dead-soft brass wire

- 6 light green 5mm oval cultured potato pearl beads (look for pearls at www.beadaholique.com)

- 4 peacock blue-gray 5mm oval cultured potato pearl beads

- 6 olive green 4mm button cultured pearl beads

- Flat nose, chain nose, and round nose pliers

- Side cutters

- Ruler (for measuring chain)

- Flat nylon jaw pliers; medium-cut, flat needle file; mandrel; chasing hammer; and steel bench block (for making ear wires)

Make the Feather Duster Earrings

1 Select 2 longer peacock feathers that are about the same length, and lie them down convex side up.

NOTE: You can trim the base of a feather with side cutters to shorten it.

2 Use a toothpick to daub a drop of white glue on each feather near the base of its shaft.

3 Select 2 slightly shorter peacock feathers that are about the same length, and stack each one on top of a longer feather from Step 1, convex side up.

2

4 Use a toothpick to daub a drop of white glue on each of the shorter peacock feathers, the same way you applied glue to the first 2 feathers, but offset them so that the stacked feathers slightly fan out.

5 Select 2 grizzly rooster feathers that are approximately the same length, and stack each one on one of the feathers from Step 4.

4

6 Use the clean end of a toothpick to gently press the feathers together with the glue.

7 Make sure that the shafts of all 3 feathers in each stack come together at their bases (which will be the top of each earring drop), and set the feathers aside.

8 Use side cutters to cut 4 segments of chain: 2 that have 16 links and 2 that have 6 links.

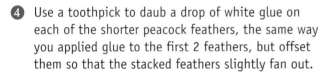

6

8

9. String a light green pearl onto one of the head pins, and use side cutters and round nose pliers to secure it with a simple connector loop.

10. Repeat this process with 5 more light green pearls, all 4 gray pearls, and all 6 olive green pearls.

11. Use flat nose or chain nose pliers to attach a light green pearl drop to one end of each of the longer chain segments.

10

12. Attach a gray pearl drop to the fourth link in from the light green drop on each longer chain segment.

13. Skip a link in each chain, and attach an olive green pearl drop.

14. Skip 2 links in each chain, and attach another light green drop; skip 1 link, and attach a gray drop; and skip 2 links, and attach an olive green drop.

15. Attach the remaining 2 olive green drops to the ends of the shorter lengths of chain.

15

16. Skip a link in each shorter chain, and attach a light green drop.

17. Use flat nose pliers to bend the wings on each fold-over clamp end inward about 45 degrees. (They are at 90 degrees when you purchase them.)

⓲ Use a toothpick to daub a drop of white glue on the inside of each clamp end.

⓳ Place the glued ends of each stack of feathers into the glue in each clamp end.

⓴ Use flat nose pliers to gently bend the wings on the clamp ends down onto the feathers.

NOTE: Don't worry if a small amount of glue oozes out; it dries clear and should not be noticeable.

㉑ Slide an open jump ring through the connector ring on one of the clamp ends.

㉒ Slide the empty link at the end of one of the longer chain segments onto the jump ring so that the chain rests against the convex side of the stacked feathers.

㉓ Slide the empty link at the end of one of the shorter chain segments onto the jump ring in front of the longer segment.

㉔ Use chain nose and flat nose pliers to close the jump ring.

㉕ Perform steps 21–24 with the second stack of feathers, the second clamp end, and the remaining 2 chain segments.

㉖ Use 20-gauge wire to make a pair of Circular French Hooks, and attach their connector loops to the jump rings. Make sure the ear wires face opposite directions.

18

20

22

23

24

26

Ravenwood Earrings

Sleek, black goose feathers create shiny accents against the grain of natural cherry wood.

Estimated time to complete: 1 hour • **Approximate length:** 3 inches

TECHNIQUES
Chapter 2

- "Straighten, Cut, and File Wire"
- "Bend, Shape, and Hammer Wire"
- "Make Jump Rings"

- "Open and Close Jump Rings"

Chapter 3

- "Bail-Maker French Hooks"

TOOLS AND MATERIALS

- 2 cherry wood 34mm fan connector chandelier parts (look for these at www.beadaholique.com)
- 2 black goose biot feathers between 5 and 8 inches long (these are sold in 2-inch strips at www.moonlightfeather.com)
- 40 inches of 28-gauge Bead Smith Tarnish Resistant Craft Wire in gold
- About 14 inches of 20-gauge, dead-soft brass wire

- Ruler (for measuring wire)
- Side cutters (the sharper the better for trimming feathers)
- Chain nose, round nose, and flat nose pliers
- Chasing hammer and steel bench block
- ¼-inch (6mm) mandrel
- Flat nylon jaw pliers; bail-making pliers; and medium-cut, flat needle file (for making ear wires)

Make the Ravenwood Earrings

1 Use your fingers to gently straighten, and then side cutters to cut, 20 inches of 28-gauge wire.

2 Thread the wire through the center bottom hole in one of the cherry wood connectors.

3 Center the wire in the hole, and bring the ends of the wire together to bend it into a long "U" shape.

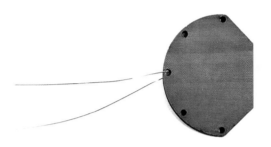

3

4 If your goose feathers are sewn together at their bases, use side cutters to trim the threads and remove 2 feathers.

5 Center a feather over the bottom of the wood connector, inside the wire "U."

6 Position the feather so that its flat side is against the edge of the connector, and hold it there with your fingers.

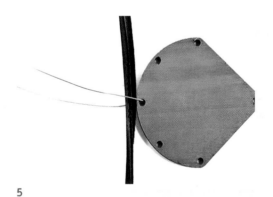

5

7 Pull one end of the wire over the feather, at an angle between feather fringes, and press the wire down against the broad side of the wood connector.

8 Pull the other end of the wire over the feather in the opposite direction, between the same fringes, and press that end down against the connector.

9 Pass one end of the wire through the center hole in the connector (again), and pull it all the way through, gently, to tighten down the second wrap of wire on the feather.

10 On the side where that wire exits the hole, cross that wire over the other end of the wire, and pass it through the next adjacent hole in the connector.

11 Press the feather against the edge of the connector above that hole.

12 Use your thumb to press the wire down against the broad side of the connector, and use your other hand to pull the wire back over the feather, and then pass the wire through the same hole again.

13 Pull the wire gently to tighten it down, and then bring it back over the feather a second time.

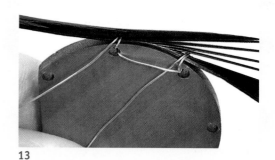

13

14 Pass the wire behind the segment of wire that runs between the first and second holes, and gently pull it taut. Feed the wire through slowly to keep it from kinking.

15 Pass the wire through the next hole, and gently pull it taut.

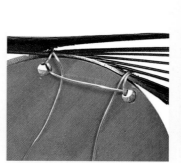

16. Press the feather down against the narrow edge of the wood connector again, and bring the wire over the feather.

17. Slowly feed the wire through the hole and back over the feather again.

18. Pass the wire beneath the wire segment that runs between the previous 2 holes.

16   18

19. Pass the wire through the top center hole in the wood connector, and pull the wire taut.

20. Gently bend the feather against the top of the connector, allowing the feather to form an arc.

21. Bring the wire over the feather.

22. Pass through the hole, and bring the wire over the feather again.

23. Pass the wire up beneath the segment of wire that runs between the previous 2 holes, and gently pull the wire taut.

22

24. Repeat Step 23 a few more times to make several wraps around the wire. The wraps do not need to be stacked tightly together. If you have trouble grasping the wire with your fingers, you can use chain nose pliers to make the wraps.

25. Press the wire down against the connector with your thumb, and then use side cutters to trim the wire close to the wraps.

26. Use chain nose pliers to squeeze down the end of the wire so that its sharp end faces the connector. (See the photo for Step 30 for an example.)

25

27. Go back to the center hole in the connector, and pass the other wire end through the next empty hole.

28. Use this end of the wire to stitch the feather onto this half of the connector, using the same process you used for the first half.

29. When you reach the top of the connector, allow the feather ends to cross, and make your wraps over both ends.

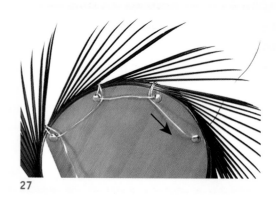

27

30. Wrap, trim, and press down the wire to end it, just like you did with the other end of the wire in steps 23–26.

31. Use side cutters to trim both ends of the feather, at an angle, about ¼ inch from the final wire wraps.

32. Repeat steps 1–31 to make a second earring drop.

33. Use 20-gauge wire and the mandrel to make 2 large jump rings.

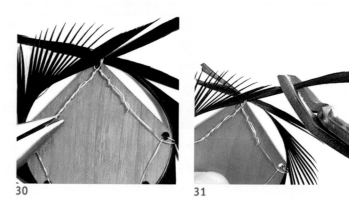

30

31

34. Open each jump ring wide, and connect it to the top hole in each connector.

35. Use the middle of the jaws of your round nose pliers to make 2 smaller jump rings with 20-gauge wire, and attach each one to a larger jump ring on the connector.

36. Make a pair of 20-gauge Bail-Maker French Hooks, and attach them to the smaller jump rings.

36

Facets and Chains Earrings

Put your wire wrapping skills to the test with these drapey earrings that feature designer Czech glass beads and layers of antiqued brass chain.

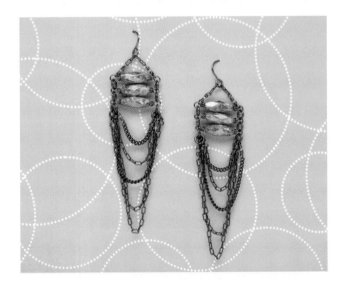

Specifications

Estimated time to complete: 1½ hours ● **Approximate length:** 3¾ inches

TECHNIQUES
Chapter 2

- "Straighten Wire"

- "Cut Wire"

- "Open and Close Simple Connector Loops"

- "Open and Close Jump Rings"

- "Wire Wrap Regular Beads"

- "Cut Closed-Link Chain"

- "Picking Up Beads"

TOOLS AND MATERIALS

- About 70 inches of 24-gauge Artistic craft wire in gunmetal or Vintaj Bronze finish

- 16 Vintaj Natural Brass 5mm jump rings

- 2 ready-made Vintaj Natural Brass 20mm x 10mm French Ear Wires

- 7 inches of Vintaj Natural Brass 2mm Delicate Curb Chain

- 38 inches of Vintaj Natural Brass 3.5mm x 2mm Fine Ornate Chain

- Flat nylon jaw pliers

- Side cutters

- Round nose, chain nose, and flat nose pliers

- 6 faceted 15mm barrel (or "spaghetti") Czech fire-polished glass beads in alabaster Picasso (or a similar color—look for these at www.etsy.com or www.ebay.com)

- 12 size 15/0 round Miyuki seed beads in matte rainbow light gold (or a similar color)

- Ruler (for measuring wire and chain)

Make the Facets and Chains Earrings

1 Use your fingers or flat nylon jaw pliers to gently straighten several inches of 24-gauge wire still on the spool.

2 String one 15mm bead.

3 Grasp the wire with round nose pliers about 2 inches from the end of the wire and make a wrapped loop with 3 wraps.

3

4 Grasp the loop with chain nose pliers, and use your fingers or the round nose pliers to wrap a second set of wraps on top of the first, from the bottom up. This is called making *double wraps*.

5 Use side cutters to trim the wire close to the wraps, and use the tips of chain nose pliers to press down the wire end.

6 Slide the bead up against the wraps, and use the round nose pliers to make a second double wrap on the other side of the bead.

7 Trim off the wire close to the wraps, and press it down with the tips of chain nose pliers.

Completed wrapped bead link

8 Perform steps 1–7 to make 2 more double-wrapped 15mm beads. Be sure to select beads that are very similar in length (actual bead lengths vary slightly).

9 Use flat nose and chain nose pliers to connect the 3 beads with 2 jump rings.

10 Arrange the beads in a "Z" formation, and use flat nose pliers to slide an open jump ring through the empty loop on one of the end beads and a loop on the middle bead, as shown.

11 Close the jump ring. Check to make sure that the jump ring lies perpendicular to the beads (like a spacer between rungs in a ladder).

12 Use the same technique to attach a fourth jump ring on the other side.

9   10

13 Straighten several inches of 24-gauge wire on the spool, and string on a seed bead. (You can use the wire like a needle to pick up the bead.)

14 Use round nose pliers to make a tiny wrapped loop with the end of the wire. (Make regular single wraps, not double wraps.)

15 Slide the seed bead against the wraps, and trim the wire off of the spool 1¹⁄₂ inches past the seed bead.

16 Use round nose pliers to begin making a second wrapped loop, but stop before you make any wraps.

16

⑰ Use side cutters to cut 2 lengths of 2mm curb chain: one that is 2½ inches long and one that is 1 inch long. Be sure to completely remove the cut links at the ends.

⑱ Slide the last link on one of the chain segments onto the unwrapped loop from Step 16.

⑲ Grasp the loop carefully with flat nose or chain nose pliers, and complete the wraps.

18

19

⑳ Trim and press down the end of the wire as usual.

㉑ Use the same technique to attach a wrapped seed bead link to the other end of the chain segment, and to each end of the other chain segment.

㉒ Cut a 2-inch length of 3.5mm chain.

㉓ String one of the end links on the chain onto 24-gauge wire still on the spool, and make a small wrapped loop at the end of the wire.

21

23

㉔ Grasp the wraps with chain nose pliers, and bend the wire about 45 degrees.

㉕ Use round nose pliers to make a second loop against the wraps, but do not make any wraps.

㉖ Slide the chain link into the loop (see the next page).

24

25

㉗ Hold the loop gently with chain nose pliers, and make 2 or 3 wraps over the first set of wraps. This is called making a *wrapped figure-eight connector.*

㉘ Trim and press down the wire as usual.

㉙ Make a second wrapped figure-eight connector on the other end of the chain.

㉚ Use a new jump ring to connect the 3 chain segments—longest to shortest—to a bottom loop on the linked beads.

㉛ Hook another jump ring through the opposite ends of all 3 chain segments, and bring them up to the loop on the opposite side of the lowest 15mm bead.

㉜ Attach this jump ring to the loop on that side. When you hold up the earring, the chains should be in opposite order on both sides so that the chains cross.

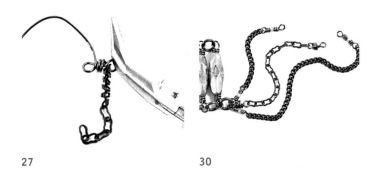

27   30

㉝ Cut 2 more lengths of 3.5mm chain: one 3¾ inches long and one 3¼ inches long.

㉞ Make and attach wrapped loop seed bead connectors to each end of the longer segment.

㉟ Make and attach wrapped figure-eight connectors to each end of the shorter segment.

34 and 35

149

36 Use a jump ring to attach these 2 new segments to the jump ring that you attached in Step 30, on the front side of the earring.

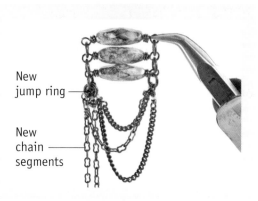

New jump ring —

New chain segments —

37 Use another jump ring to attach the opposite ends of both segments to the jump ring that you attached in Step 31, on the back side of the earring. (Doing so causes the chain segments to cross from front to back.)

38 Cut 2 more segments of 3.5mm with just 2 chain links each.

39 Begin making another wrapped seed bead connector, but stop before making any wraps.

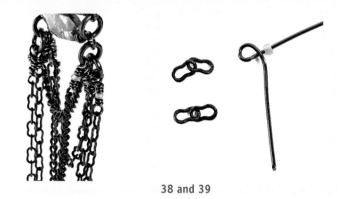

37   38 and 39

40 Slide a link from one of the short chain segments into the loop on the connector, and then make the first set of wraps.

41 Make the second loop on the connector, but do not make the wraps.

42 Slide one of the wrapped loops at the top of the earring into the unwrapped loop on the connector.

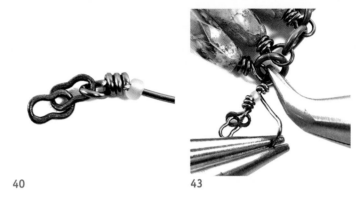

43 Make the wraps (see photo) and trim and squeeze down the wire end, as usual.

40   43

44 Make another wrapped seed bead connector and use it to link the other short chain segment to the upper loop on the other side of the earring.

45 Use chain nose pliers to open the ring on one of the ear wires.

46 Slide the loose ends of both short chain segments onto the ring.

47 Close the ring to complete the first earring.

44   47

48 Repeat steps 1–47 to make a second, matching earring.

CHAPTER 7

Rugged Details

This chapter features designs that are whimsical, edgy, industrial, and truly unique. Their components range from ready-made findings to reclaimed mechanical parts.

Bounty Saber Chandeliers

Tiny silver sabers and showy black roses give these earrings a light-hearted air of pirate chic.

Specifications

Estimated time to complete: 20 minutes • **Approximate length:** 2¼ inches

TECHNIQUES

Chapter 2

- "Open and Close Simple Connector Loops"
- "Open and Close Jump Rings"
- "Wire Wrap a Briolette or Teardrop Bead"

Chapter 3

- "Bail-Maker French Hooks"

TOOLS AND MATERIALS

- 2 Vintaj Arte Metal 38mm Blooming Flower pendants
- 10 antiqued silver-plated JBB 13mm saber charms (try www.rings-things.com)
- 10 Artistic Wire 18-gauge, 5.56mm chain maille jump rings in black
- 2 gunmetal, 5mm x 4mm oval, 20-gauge gunmetal jump rings
- 2 bright red, 9mm x 6mm briolette glass beads (sometimes sold as "red quartz")

- 24 inches of 26-gauge, dead-soft, round sterling silver or silver-filled wire
- About 4 inches of 20-gauge, dead-soft, round sterling silver or silver-filled wire
- Ruler (for measuring wire)
- 1.25mm round hole punching pliers
- Round nose pliers
- 2 pairs of chain nose pliers
- Flat nylon jaw pliers; bail-making pliers; side cutters; medium-cut, flat needle file; chasing hammer; and steel bench block (for making ear wires)

Make the Bounty Saber Chandeliers

1 Use hole punching pliers to punch holes near the center of each of the bottom 5 petals on one of the flower pendants.

2 Use chain nose pliers to attach a saber charm on a 5.56mm jump ring to each hole that you just pierced. Position the charms so that the tips of the sabers curve toward the center line of the flower, as shown.

3 Use your fingers to gently straighten 12 inches of 26-gauge wire, and use side cutters to cut it from the spool.

2

4 String on one of the briolettes, and use the wire to wrap its top.

5 Use hole punching pliers to pierce another hole in the flower pendant, just above the hole that you previously punched in the bottom petal on the far left.

Bounty Saber Chandeliers *(continued)*

6 Attach the wrapped briolette to the flower by sliding it onto an oval jump ring and attaching the jump ring to the hole that you just punched.

7 Repeat steps 1–6 to make a second earring drop for your pair.

6

8 Use 20-gauge wire to make a pair of Bail-Maker French Hooks.

9 Attach each ear wire to the ready-made pierced hole at the top of each flower. Make sure that the unlooped end of each wire points toward the back of each earring.

9

TIP

Embellishing flower pendants with resin

You can make the Bounty Saber Chandeliers more colorful by applying colored epoxy resin to some of the flowers' petals before assembling your earrings. Just be sure to leave the areas where you need to pierce holes resin free.

See the book *More Teach Yourself VISUALLY Jewelry Making* for detailed instructions on preparing and applying resin.

A flower pendant coated with colored resin

Hands of Time Earrings

Repurposed clock hands and ready-made gears give these convertible earrings a gritty steampunk look.

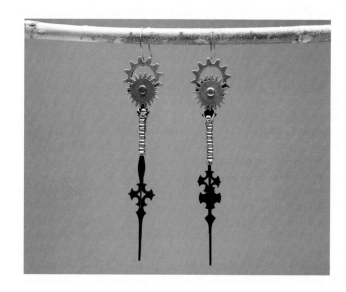

Specifications

Estimated time to complete: 30 minutes • **Approximate length:** 5 inches

TECHNIQUES

Chapter 2

- "Straighten, Cut, and File Wire"
- "Bend, Shape, and Hammer Wire"
- "Open and Close Simple Connector Loops"

- "Wire Wrap a Briolette or Teardrop Bead"
- "Wrap Wire"

Chapter 3

- "Circular French Hooks"

TOOLS AND MATERIALS

- About 30 inches of 24-gauge Artistic Wire in gunmetal or Vintaj bronze
- Side cutters for up to 14-gauge wire
- Flat nose, chain nose, and round nose pliers
- 4 reclaimed metal clock hands, 2 longer and 2 shorter
- About 3 inches of 3mm stainless steel ball chain
- 2 gears and 2 open cogwheels from the Tim Holtz idea-ology Sprocket Gears pack

- 2 Tim Holtz idea-ology long fasteners
- About 4 inches of 21-gauge, half-hard, round antiqued bronze wire
- Flat needle file; mandrel; medium-cut, flat needle file; chasing hammer; and steel bench block (for making Circular French Hooks)

*The clock hands used in the example range from about 2¹⁄₂ to 3³⁄₄ inches in length. They were purchased from Gatherer of Great Things at www.etsy.com/shop/gatherergreatthings.

Make the Hands of Time Earrings

① Use your fingers to gently straighten, and then side cutters to cut, about 15 inches of 24-gauge wire.

② Use flat nose pliers to bend about 1 inch of the wire to create a narrow "U."

③ Stack one of the shorter clock hands on top of one of the longer clock hands, with the holes at the tops of the hands aligned. Check first to see which side of each hand is intended to face up; the edges should look smoother on that side.

3

④ Hook the wire "U" over both clock hands just above their bottom ornamentation, with the short tail of wire on the bottom side of the hands.

⑤ Holding the wire tail for leverage, make 3 tight wraps around the clock hands.

⑥ Lay your ball chain next to the clock hands, and count the number of balls it will take to cover the clock hands from the bottom adornments to just below the top adornments. (If the chain turns out to be slightly too long, you can trim it after Step 10.)

5

⑦ Use heavy side cutters to cut that length of ball chain.

⑧ Hold the chain segment on top of the clock hands, just above the 3 initial wire wraps.

⑨ Use your free hand to wrap the wire over the connector between the bottom 2 balls on the chain, and all the way around the clock hands, twice.

9

10. Working your way up the clock hands, make 2 wraps around each connector link in the chain, except for the very last connector.

11. Make a single wrap over that last connector link.

12. Make a second wrap over the same link, but bring the wire up diagonally over the upper ornamentation on the clock hand, as shown.

11

12

13. Bring the wire around the back of the hands, and then down diagonally below the last ball in the chain segment.

14. Wrap the wire up diagonally again (on top of the wrap from Step 12), and make 3 tight wraps around the clock hands just above the upper ornamentation.

15. Use side cutters to trim both wire tails on the back of the clock hands, and use the tips of chain nose pliers to press them down.

16. Stack a gear and a cogwheel over the tops of the clock hands, as shown. Make sure that the fronts face up (the fronts are smoother than the backs).

17. Slide a long fastener through the holes in the gear, cogwheel, and both clock hands, front to back. In the example, an antiqued brass tone fastener is used to contrast with the silver tone gear.

18. Use your fingers to bend the 2 tabs on the fastener away from each other and against the clock hands.

19. Pull the open cogwheel toward the top of the earring drop as far as it will go.

19

20. Repeat steps 1–19 to make a second earring drop. Be aware that if your clock hands are not identical, your earring drops won't be identical either. In the example, contrasting colors of Tim Holtz components are used to accentuate the differences.

㉑ Use 21-gauge wire to make a pair of Circular French Hooks with loops large enough to connect to the open cogwheels on the earring drops.

㉒ Use chain nose pliers to attach the ear wires to the drops.

22

The completed earrings can be worn in two ways: with the clock hands (a) or as simple cogwheel drops (b).

a

To temporarily remove the open cogwheels and wear them alone, slide each cogwheel backward over the gear wheel and over the tops of the stacked clock hands (c). Continue sliding the cogwheel all the way down the clock hands and off of the earring drop. Reverse this process to replace each cogwheel.

b

c

Kyanite Gem Sticks

Kyanite gem sticks are reflective, roughly hewn shards of denim blue stone. Showcase them with these silver earrings that feature built-in hook ear wires.

Estimated time to complete: 35 minutes ● **Approximate length:** 2¼ inches

TECHNIQUES

Chapter 2

- "Straighten, Cut, and File Wire"
- "Bend, Shape, and Hammer Wire"
- "Make Simple Connector Loops"

- "Open and Close Simple Connector Loops"

Chapter 3

- "Circular French Hooks"

TOOLS AND MATERIALS

- 1 strand of kyanite gem stick pendants (look for these at www.beadaholique.com)
- 3½ inches of 18-gauge, dead-soft, round sterling silver wire
- 5 inches of 20-gauge, dead-soft, round sterling silver wire
- 10 sterling silver 2mm x 2mm crimp tubes
- ¾-inch mandrel (a wooden dowel was used for the example)
- Jewelry polishing cloth

- Flat nylon jaw pliers
- Side cutters
- Chain nose, flat nose, and round nose pliers
- Bracelet-bending pliers
- Bail-making pliers
- Medium-cut, flat needle file
- Bead reamer and bowl of water
- Chasing hammer and steel bench block

Make the Kyanite Gem Sticks

1 Use flat nylon jaw pliers to straighten a few inches of 18-gauge wire still on its spool.

2 Pull the wire through a jewelry polishing cloth several times to polish it.

3 Use side cutters to flush-cut a 1¾-inch segment of the wire.

4 Flat-file both ends of the wire with a needle file.

5 Use round nose pliers to make a small loop at one end of the wire.

5

6 Use bracelet-bending pliers to curve the entire length of the wire segment, beginning with the looped end. Press the loop sideways between the jaws of the pliers, and repeat this process along the wire, one short segment at a time, to create a smooth curve.

7 Unstring all the kyanite pendants on your strand, and lay them out on your work surface.

8 Select 2 sets of 4 pendants, one for each earring in your pair.

9. Dip the tip of the bead reamer into a bowl of water, and then insert it into the drill hole on one of the pendants you selected.

10. Using gentle force, twist the reamer back and forth to enlarge the hole. As the hole becomes larger, it will slide farther up on the reamer.

11. Turn the kyanite around, and ream the hole from the other side.

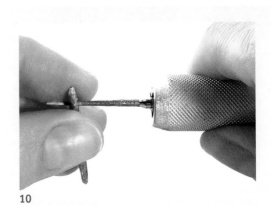

10

12. Test the hole size by attempting to slide it onto the 18-gauge wire segment. If the hole is too small, continue reaming until it is just large enough to fit. Remove the kyanite from the wire when you are finished.

13. Repeat this process to ream the remaining 7 kyanite pendants.

12

14. Slide a crimp tube onto the 18-gauge wire segment.

15. Slide on each of the 4 kyanite pendants for the first earring, spacing each pendant with a single crimp tube.

16. Slide on 1 more crimp tube.

16

⑰ Use round nose pliers to make a small loop at the straight end of the wire segment. Make this loop about the same size, and facing in the same direction, as the first loop.

⑱ Use flat nose pliers to gently bend each loop upward 90 degrees, as shown.

⑲ Use your fingers to center the kyanite pendants and the crimp tubes on the wire, and then use chain nose pliers to squeeze the first and last crimp tubes against the wire. Use as much force as you can so that these 2 crimps remain in place.

⑳ Straighten and polish a few inches of 20-gauge wire, and flush-cut a 2½-inch segment.

㉑ Flat-file one end of the wire.

㉒ Use round nose pliers to make a small loop at that end.

㉓ Use bail-making pliers to bend the other end of the wire, as shown. Bend the wire around the larger barrel of the pliers, and roll them in the same direction that you rolled the loop at the other end of the wire.

㉔ Use the needle file to debur this end.

23

165

25 Center the wire on the mandrel, and bend the wire into a large "U" in the opposite direction that you rolled the end loop and the bend.

26 Use a chasing hammer and bench block to slightly flatten the large curve in the wire. Hammer until the wire is stiff enough to hold its shape as an ear wire.

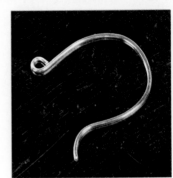

27 Use chain nose pliers to attach the looped end of the 20-gauge wire to one of the loops on the 18-gauge wire with the kyanite. The larger "U" in the 20-gauge wire should be upside down and extend over the tops of the kyanite.

28 Slide the other end of the 20-gauge wire through the other loop on the 18-gauge wire to secure the ear wire and complete the first earring. Use your fingers or bail-making pliers to make any needed adjustments in the shape of the 20-gauge wire.

29 Repeat steps 1–6 and steps 14–28 to complete the second earring using the other set of 4 kyanite pendants that you previously reamed.

These steel hoop drops are bold yet comfortable to wear.

Specifications

Estimated time to complete: 50 minutes   •   **Approximate length:** 3½ inches

TECHNIQUES

Chapter 2

- "Straighten, Cut, and File Wire"

- "Bend, Shape, and Hammer Wire"

- "Make and Use Simple Connector Loops and Jump Rings"

- "Wrap Wire Over Wire"

- "Wire Wrap a Briolette or Teardrop Bead"

- "Create a Patina with Liver of Sulfur"

Chapter 3

- "Circular French Hooks"

TOOLS AND MATERIALS

- About 35 inches of 18-gauge, round, dark annealed steel wire*
- About 16 feet of 28-gauge, round, dark annealed steel wire*
- About 4 inches of 20-gauge, dead-soft, round sterling silver wire
- Ruler (for measuring wire)
- Flat nylon jaw pliers
- Side cutters for up to 14-gauge wire
- Medium-cut, flat needle file
- Chain nose, flat nose, and round nose pliers

- 2-inch round mandrel (a toothpick jar was used for the example)
- Steel bristle brush
- 2 obsidian black gem-faceted 13mm briolettes (look for these at www.beadaholique.com)
- Steel bench block, small mandrel, and chasing hammer (for making Circular French Hooks)
- Liver of sulfur and related supplies for creating a patina (see Chapter 2)

*The wire used in the example was purchased at www.dickblick.com. Although this wire is labeled "18-gauge wire," it is often closer to 17-gauge (which is slightly thicker).

Make the Quarantine Hoops

① Unwind about 16 inches of 18-gauge wire from its coil or spool, and use flat nylon jaw pliers to straighten it as best you can. (Steel wire is more difficult to straighten than nonferrous—non-iron-containing—metal wire.)

② Use side cutters to flush-cut the end of the wire and flush-cut 16 inches of wire from the coil or spool.

③ Flat file both ends of the wire.

④ Working with the 28-gauge wire still on the spool, use flat nose pliers to bend the last inch of the wire into a narrow "U."

5

⑤ Slide the wire "U" over the 18-gauge wire 2 inches from one end, and make 3 tight wraps.

⑥ Using the short wire tail for leverage, begin making more wraps around the 18-gauge wire, this time spacing them about $1/16$ inch apart.

⑦ Continue making spaced wraps until only 1 inch of unwrapped 18-gauge wire remains at the other end. (You can allow the spool of 28-gauge wire to hang down toward the ground while you make the wraps.)

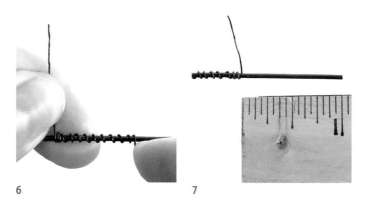

6   7

⑧ Turn the 18-gauge wire around, and begin making spaced wraps in the opposite direction, on top of the first wraps. Make the new wraps at opposing angles to the first wraps so that they cross.

8

169

⑨ Keep wrapping until you reach the beginning of the first wraps.

NOTE: While you make wraps, some black coating may rub off on your fingers; it will wash off with soap and water.

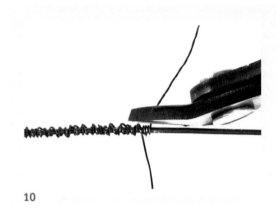

⑩ Use side cutters to trim the short, 28-gauge tail (see photo), and use the tips of chain nose pliers to press it down.

⑪ Returning to the spool end of the 28-gauge wire, make 3 tight wraps on top of the first 3 wraps you made to start the initial wraps.

10

⑫ Trim the 28-gauge wire close to the wraps, and use the tips of chain nose pliers to press down that end.

⑬ Wrap the 18-gauge wire around the mandrel twice, until the ends cross, as shown.

⑭ Remove the wire from the mandrel, and use your fingers to gently bring the ends toward one another until they cross at the point where the wraps begin and end.

⑮ Wrap the 2 inches of unwrapped wire at the end over and around the doubled wire, as shown. Make 2 complete wraps. In the photo, chain nose pliers are being used to make them.

⑯ After completing the 2 wraps, use side cutters to trim the wire on the inside of the hoop with a flush-cut.

⑰ Use chain nose pliers to press down the trimmed end.

⑱ Use round nose pliers to roll the remaining tail of 18-gauge wire into a loop.

⑲ Brush the entire hoop with a steel bristle brush to back off some of the dark coating and reveal the bright steel beneath it.

A completed hoop

20. Gently straighten and then cut a 21-inch length of 28-gauge wire.

21. Use that wire to wrap one of the briolettes.

22. Use the largest part of the jaws of your chain nose pliers to make an 18-gauge jump ring.

23. Brush the wire on the briolette and the jump ring with the steel bristle brush to partially back off their color.

23

24. Use flat nose and chain nose pliers to attach the jump ring to the loop on the briolette.

25. Open the loop on the hoop, and slide on the jump ring.

26. Close the loop with the jump ring attached completely below it, as shown.

27. Repeat steps 1–26 to make a second wrapped hoop.

25   26

28. Use 20-gauge sterling silver wire to make a pair of Circular French Hooks.

29. Use liver of sulfur to create a dark patina on the ear wires, and do not back off the color with steel wool. Be sure to immerse only the sterling ear wires in the liver of sulfur, and not your steel hoops; the steel is not stainless and can rust easily if exposed to moisture.

30. When the hooks are completely dry, attach them to the hoops so that the front sides of both earrings face forward when you wear them. Always keep your earrings dry to protect the steel from rust.

Spiky Scribe Drops

G et noticed with these earrings made from reclaimed mechanical pencil heads wrapped with glass spikes.

Specifications

Estimated time to complete: 40 minutes ● **Approximate length:** 2½ inches

TECHNIQUES

Chapter 2

- "Straighten, Cut, and File Wire"

- "Bend, Shape, and Hammer Wire"

- "Open and Close Simple Connector Loops"

- "Wrap Wire Over Wire"

Chapter 3

- "Bail-Maker French Hooks"

TOOLS AND MATERIALS

- 2 reclaimed mechanical pencil tips

- About 28 inches of 24-gauge Artistic Wire in gunmetal or Vintaj bronze

- About 32 inches of 28-gauge, dead-soft, round brass wire

- About 4 inches of 22-gauge, dead-soft, round brass wire

- 6 glass 2mm x 6mm spike beads in magical raspberry (look for these at www.bellomodo.com)

- Chain nose and round nose pliers

- Side cutters

- Ruler (for measuring wire)

- Flat nylon jaw pliers; bail-making pliers; medium-cut, flat needle file; chasing hammer; and steel bench block (for making ear wires)

*The pencil tips in the example were purchased from Ferrera at www.etsy.com/shop/Ferrera.

Make the Spiky Scribe Drops

1 Use chain nose pliers to flatten the tube of metal at the back end of one of the pencil tips. (This step is optional, but it makes the end of the pencil look slightly neater.)

2 If your pencil contains a lead (graphite), twist its body and cone cap until the lead is fully extruded, and then remove it from the pencil.

3 Use your fingers to gently straighten, and then side cutters to cut, about 14 inches of 24-gauge wire.

4 Slide one end of the wire down into the bottom of the spiral groove in the pencil mechanism. It should slide in far enough that about ½ inch of the wire is hidden within the cone end of the pencil.

4

5 Make 2 complete, tight wraps around the pencil at the base of its twist mechanism. Use the same technique you use to wrap wire over wire.

6 String on one of the spike beads, and position it about ¼ inch from the wraps.

7 Press the base of the spike against the pencil, and make 2 more wraps.

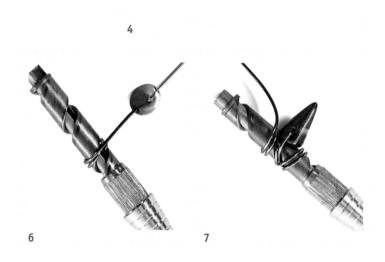

6

7

8. String on a second glass spike, and position it about ¼ inch from the wraps.

9. Press the base of the spike against the pencil, and make 2 more wraps.

10. Use the same method to wrap a third spike onto the pencil.

11. Keep making wire wraps around the pencil until you reach its end.

12. Use chain nose pliers to bend back the wire 90 degrees, as shown.

12

13. Bend the wire over the end of the pencil.

14. Grasp the wire with round nose pliers at the center point of the pencil end, and wrap the wire around the pliers to make a loop.

15. Gently hold the loop with chain nose pliers, and use your other hand to wrap the wire back down around the pencil at least 3 times. Do so gently and deliberately so that the wire wraps around the pencil rather than springing off the end.

16. Use side cutters to trim off the wire tail close to the wraps.

17. Use the tips of chain nose pliers to gently press down the wire end.

15

18 Use your fingers to gently straighten, and side cutters to cut, about 16 inches of 28-gauge wire.

19 Slide one end of the wire into the same groove that you slid the beginning of the 24-gauge wire, but in the *opposite* direction; push the wire end toward the back end of the pencil rather than toward the cone tip.

19

20 Make several wraps around the pencil, moving toward the wraps of 24-gauge wire.

21 Bring the wire under and then all the way around the first spike, near its base. Hold the wire down around the base of the spike as you make the wrap.

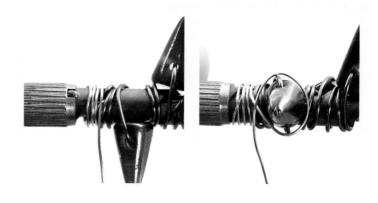

22 Make a second wrap around the spike just above the first. Again, use your fingers to guide the position of the wrap as you make it.

23 Wrap the wire all the way around the pencil, moving toward the second spike.

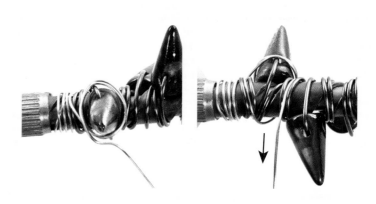

㉔ Wrap the wire up and around the base of the second spike twice, the same way you wrapped the first spike.

㉕ Wrap the wire all the way around the pencil, and then up and around the base of the third spike twice.

㉖ Wrap the wire around the pencil, on top of the 24-gauge wraps, 2 or 3 times, moving toward the end of the pencil.

㉗ Make 3 or 4 wraps around the base of the loop in the 24-gauge wire.

㉘ Use side cutters to trim the 28-gauge wire close to the wraps.

㉙ Use chain nose pliers to gently press down the wire end.

27

29

㉚ Repeat steps 1–29 to make a second, matching earring drop.

㉛ Use 22-gauge wire to make a pair of Bail-Maker French Hooks. In the example, the unlooped sides of the hooks were pulled gently downward to elongate them.

㉜ Use chain nose pliers to attach each spiky drop to an ear wire.

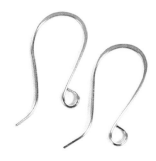

31

32

CHAPTER 8

Retro Chic Designs

These earrings invoke the styles of decades past, with elegant florals, romantic pearls, and beaded clusters.

Gilded Posies Earrings

Let your inner fine artist shine through as you hand-paint the "gilding" on these vintage-style Lucite flowers.

Specifications

Estimated time to complete: 30 minutes (plus 12–24 hours of glue drying time) ● **Approximate length:** 2½ inches

TECHNIQUES

Chapter 2

- "Straighten, Cut, and File Wire"
- "Bend, Shape, and Hammer Wire"
- "Open and Close Simple Connector Loops"

Chapter 3

- "Bracelet-Bender Marquise Wires"

TOOLS AND MATERIALS

- 2 Lucite posy bouquet cabochons in your choice of color (the example uses matte pink and white two-tone)*
- Lumiere metallic acrylic craft paint in Super Copper and Metallic Bronze
- Glass or ceramic dish
- Sponge-tip applicators (look in the makeup aisle or at craft stores that sell alcohol inks)
- Toothpicks
- Glossy, clear acrylic spray sealant (such as Krylon)

- Disposable piece of cardboard
- 2 small, gold-plated Aanraku glue-on earring bails*
- E6000 glue with a precision applicator tip
- About 4 inches of dead-soft, 20-gauge, round red brass wire
- Bracelet-bending pliers; round nose pliers; medium-cut, flat needle file; chasing hammer; and steel bench block (for making ear wires)
- Chain nose pliers

*Look for posies and bails at www.beadaholique.com.

Make the Gilded Posy Earrings

1 After shaking each Lumiere paint bottle well, pour a small amount of both colors into a glass or ceramic dish. (Do not mix the colors.)

2 Dip a sponge-tip applicator into the copper paint lightly, and wipe it on the dish to remove any excess paint.

3 Use the applicator to lightly stamp the edges of the posies on one of the Lucite cabochons.

1

3

4 Optionally, daub the leaves at the bottom of the bouquet to paint them more thickly.

5 Dip a toothpick into the copper paint and use it like a paint brush to paint the lines between petals and the centers of the flowers. You can also use the toothpick to fill in the color on the leaves.

6 Dip a second toothpick into the bronze paint, and paint on highlights wherever you see fit.

7 Repeat steps 2–6 to paint the second cabochon.

5

6

181

⑧ Wash the dish with dish soap and water, and set the cabochons aside to dry. (Lumiere paint usually dries to the touch within a half-hour.)

⑨ Take the cabochons outdoors or to a well-ventilated area and set them on a piece of cardboard.

⑩ After shaking the acrylic sealer can well, use broad, sweeping strokes to lightly spray the top surfaces of both cabochons.

⑪ Apply 2 more coats of acrylic spray, allowing at least 10 minutes of drying time between coats.

The cabochons with 3 coats of sealer

⑫ Set the cabochons aside to dry for another 6–12 hours.

⑬ Apply E6000 to the pads on the earrings bails, and press them onto the backs of the cabochons, as shown. Hold each bail against each cabochon for 20–30 seconds.

⑭ Allow the E6000 to cure for at least 24 hours.

13

⑮ Use brass wire to make a pair of Bracelet-Bender Marquise Wires. Hammer them well to flatten them slightly and increase their temper.

⑯ Use chain nose pliers to attach the ring on each ear-ring bail to the connector loop on each ear wire.

Lucite posy bouquet cabochons are available in a range of pastel colors. You can use the same colors of Lumiere paint (copper and bronze) to give them a similar gilded look. The second color of posies shown are turquoise blue and white two-tone.

Pearls and Filigree Earrings

These daring earrings showcase Victorian-inspired pearls and layered, antiqued-brass filigree.

Specifications

Estimated time to complete: 40 minutes • **Approximate length:** 2³/₄ inches

TECHNIQUES

Chapter 2

- "Cut Wire"
- "Bend Wire"

- "Open and Close Simple Connector Loops"
- "Wrap Wire"

TOOLS AND MATERIALS

- 2 Vintaj Natural Brass 20mm round filigree beads
- 2 Vintaj Natural Brass 59mm clover petal filigrees
- 2 Vintaj 12mm x 10mm French Ear Wires
- Chain nose pliers
- Flat nylon jaw pliers
- Side cutters

- 6 feet of 28-gauge, tarnish-resistant, gold-tone, round craft wire
- 4 feet of 24-gauge, round Artistic Wire in gunmetal or Vintaj bronze
- 82 round 4mm glass pearl beads in vanilla or cream*
- 40 Czech glass 2mm round pearl beads in off-white*

*Look for glass pearls at www.shipwreckbeads.com.

Make the Pearls and Filigree Earrings

① Use the tips of chain nose pliers to gently pry up the end of a lobe on one of the filigree beads.

② Bend back that lobe until you have enough space to grasp it with nylon jaw pliers.

③ Use the nylon jaw pliers to gently bend the lobe up about 90 degrees, as shown.

1

3

④ Use the nylon jaw pliers to bend back the remaining 3 lobes so that the bead is completely open.

⑤ Pull and cut 3 feet of 28-gauge wire.

⑥ Starting at the base of the one of the lobes, use the wire to make 3 tight wraps around the edge of the filigree.

4

6

TIP

Use pearls with a vintage look

To create a true vintage look with your designs, look for genuine pearls or glass pearl beads that are slightly off-white, rather than pure white, and that have high *luster* (noticeable brilliance and reflectivity).

7 String one 4mm pearl, and hold it against the filigree.

8 Pass the wire down through the next hole in the filigree and then back up against its outside edge.

9 Repeat this process to stitch on 1 pearl for each hole in the filigree along this side of the filigree lobe, for a total of 5 pearls.

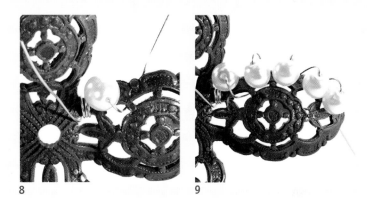

8

9

10 Turn the filigree over and pass the wire up through the next hole at the end of the lobe. Hold the last bead that you attached with one hand, and use your other hand to pull the wire taut.

11 String another pearl, and hold it against the filigree.

12 Pass the wire down over the edge of the filigree and then up through the next hole.

10

13 Repeat this process to attach beads all the way down this side of the lobe.

14 At the bottom of the lobe, wrap the wire 3 times to match the initial 3 wraps you made when you began.

15 Pass the wire down through the bottom hole in the next lobe.

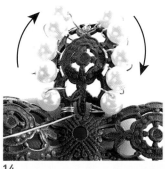

14

15

16. String on a pearl, and pull the wire taut.

17. Attach the pearl by passing down through the next hole in this lobe of the filigree.

18. Attach 4 more pearls to cover this side of the lobe.

19. At the top of the lobe, reverse direction the same way you did with the first lobe, and then attach 5 pearls down the other side. As always when wrapping wire, use your fingers to keep the wire from kinking (to the extent possible) when you make wraps.

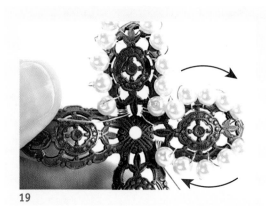

19

20. Continue this process to attach 5 pearls to each side of the remaining 2 lobes, and then use side cutters to trim off the short tail of wire where you began wrapping.

21. After completing the fourth lobe with a set of 3 wraps, turn the filigree over and pass the wire across the center of the filigree.

22. Bring the wire back up to the front of the filigree, and string two 2mm beads, one 4mm pearl, and two more 2mm beads.

21

23. Wrap the wire around the back of the filigree again, and bring it back up on the other side of the center.

24. String four 2mm beads and pass down through the first hole in one of the lobes on the opposite side of the filigree.

25. Bring the wire back up through the nearest hole in the adjacent lobe.

23

25

26 Pick up 4 more 2mm beads, and wrap the wire around the back of the filigree again.

27 Repeat steps 24–26 to attach 2 sets of four 2mm beads to the other side of the center of the filigree.

28 On the back, wrap the wire tightly around the wires that cross the center of the filigree.

NOTE: It helps to bend the very end of the wire so that you can hook it beneath the bundle of wires crossing the center.

29 Use side cutters to trim off the wire tail.

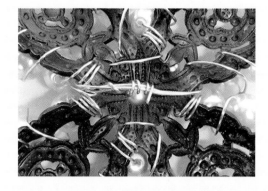

30 Cut a 6-inch length of 24-gauge wire.

31 Use your fingers to bend it into a long "U" shape.

32 Stack the beaded filigree on top of one of the 59mm clover filigrees, and align each lobe on the beaded filigree between 2 lobes on the unbeaded filigree.

33 Pass the ends of the 24-gauge wire through 2 matching holes at the end of one of the lobes on the beaded filigree.

33

34 Pass the wire ends through the nearest 2 holes on the adjacent lobes of unbeaded filigree.

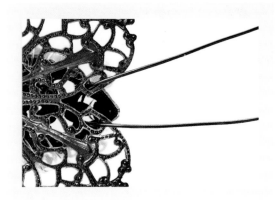

Back view

35 One at a time, wrap each wire end around the edge of the unbeaded filigree 3 or 4 times. (Use chain nose pliers if the wire slips through your fingers.) These wraps do not need to be even or neat; they are purely functional.

36 Use side cutters to trim both wire tails.

37 Use chain nose pliers to squeeze down both wire ends.

A set of wraps completed

38 Repeat steps 30–37 with each of the remaining 3 lobes of beaded filigree.

39 Use chain nose pliers to connect a ready-made ear wire to one corner of the unbeaded filigree.

40 Repeat steps 1–39 to make a second, matching earring.

40

Beaded Pinwheel Clip-Ons

A swirl of beaded cagework and aqua glass briolettes adorn these vintage-style clip backs.

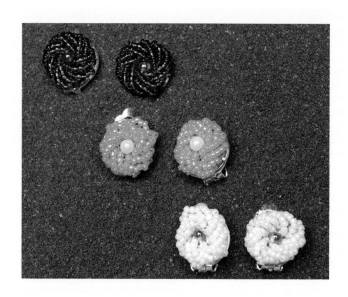

Specifications

Estimated time to complete: 30 minutes ● **Approximate diameter:** ½ inch

TECHNIQUES

Chapter 2

- "Pulling and Cutting Beading Thread"
- "Threading a Beading Needle"
- "Positioning the Needle"

- "Using a Stop Bead"
- "Picking Up Beads"
- "How to Read a Bead Key"
- "Common Beadwork Terms"

TOOLS AND MATERIALS

- 6 feet of 6-pound FireLine beading thread in crystal
- Ruler (for measuring thread)
- Size 10 beading needle
- 2 pronged, 13mm flat-pad, silver-plated clip-on earring backs*
- 2 perforated 12mm silver-plated disc findings*
- About 2½ grams of size 15/0 round Miyuki seed beads; the example uses opaque luster light cream (**A**)

- 2 magatama 3mm beads or 3.4mm drop beads; the example uses gold-lined rainbow aqua (**B**)
- 4 size 11/0 round seed beads in any color (for anchoring thread on the backs of the discs)
- Prong pusher
- Chain nose pliers
- Heavy side cutters (for up to 14-gauge wire)
- Instant bond glue

*Look for clip-ons and perforated discs at www.firemountaingems.com.

189

Make the Beaded Pinwheel Clip-Ons

1 Pull and cut 3 feet of FireLine with side cutters.

2 Thread the needle, and string on a size 11/0 seed bead.

3 Position the bead about 4 inches from the loose end of the thread, and tie a square knot over the bead to secure it (see the FAQ "How do I make a square knot in beading thread?" in Chapter 2).

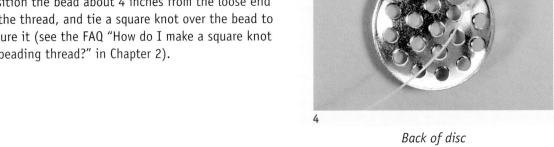

4

Back of disc

4 Pass up through one of the outermost holes on the concave side of a perforated disc, and pull the bead up against the back of the disc.

5 Pick up 10A and pass down through the indicated hole on the convex side of the disc; also see a in the diagram on the next page.

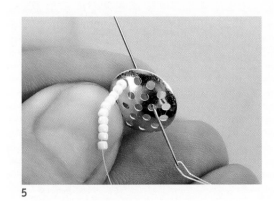

5

6 Pull the thread taut and pass up through a hole that is adjacent to the first hole in the outermost circle of holes on the disc.

7 Pick up 10A and pass down through the same hole that you passed through in Step 5; also see b in the diagram on the next page.

8 Pull the thread taut again.

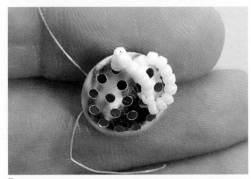

7

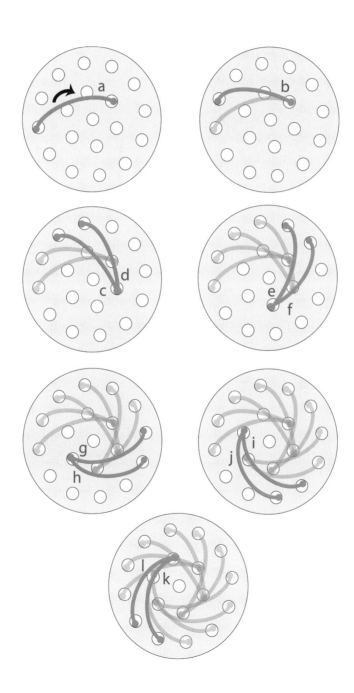

9 Pass up through the next adjacent hole in the outer circle of holes on the disc.

10 Pick up another 10A.

11 Pass down through the next hole in the middle circle of holes; also see c in the diagram on the previous page. Use your fingers to stack the new strand of 10 beads next to the previous strand, as shown.

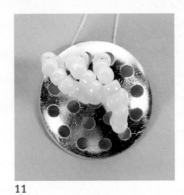

11   12

12 Pass up through the next adjacent outer hole, pick up 10A, and pass down through the same inner hole that you passed through in Step 11; also see d in the diagram on the previous page. Again, use your fingers to stack the new strand next to the previous strand.

The first 5 strands of 10A   *The first 6 strands of 10A*

13 Continue this process to stitch strands of 10A (e through l in the diagram on the previous page) all the way around the top of the disc. Notice that each strand begins in its own outer hole, but each pair of strands shares the same inner hole.

NOTE: If you feel like you have lost your place, it may help to look at the back of the disc and examine the thread paths.

All 12 strands of 10A

⑭ Turn over the disc and tie a square knot with both thread ends (the working end of the thread and the tail that you left when you started) against the back of the disc. (You do not need to remove the size 11/0 bead first, like you would with a stop bead.)

⑮ Optionally, apply a tiny drop of instant bond glue to the knot. Doing so can help keep the thread secure, but is usually unnecessary if your square knot is tight.

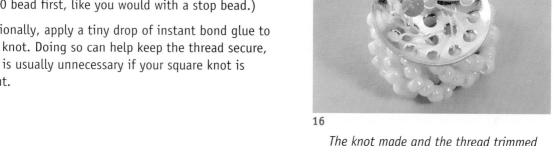

16

The knot made and the thread trimmed

⑯ Use side cutters to trim both ends of thread a few millimeters from the square knot.

⑰ Using the needle that is still on the thread that you trimmed off, pass up through the center hole in the disc, from the back side toward the front.

⑱ Center the disc on the thread, and pick up 1B.

⑲ Pass back down through the center hole in the disc.

19

⑳ Pick up a size 11/0 bead.

㉑ Pull both ends of the thread taut at the same time, and tie them in square knot.

㉒ Apply a tiny drop of instant bond glue to the knot.

㉓ Use side cutters to trim both thread ends a few millimeters from the knot.

23

The second knot tied and trimmed

㉔ Open the clip on the back of one of the clip-on earring findings.

㉕ Place the beaded disc on the front of the flat pad on the finding.

㉖ Hold the disc and the pad between your index finger and thumb, and slowly bend down each prong on the earring back with the end of the prong pusher. You do not need to press the prongs down all the way at this point; just make initial bends to get them started. Be careful not to crush any beads.

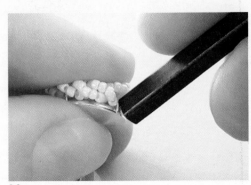

26

㉗ Use chain nose pliers to bend each prong all the way down onto the disc. Again, be careful not to crush any of the beads.

㉘ Use heavy side cutters to trim off the small metal connector ring on the clip-on's pad. Be sure to aim the connector ring away from your face when you make the cut. (Just like when you cut wire, it is a good idea to wear safety glasses.)

㉙ Repeat steps 1–28 to make a second, matching earring.

You can make these earrings in many different colors. However, because the actual dimensions of size 15/0 beads vary, your pinwheels may be tighter or looser depending on the color you use. You can adjust the look by using slightly more or fewer beads in each stitch.

Hydrangea Clip-Ons

This design takes a slightly different approach to beaded cagework, with tiny blossoms stitched individually to a perforated disc.

Specifications

Estimated time to complete: 40 minutes (plus 24 hours for glue to cure) ● **Approximate diameter:** ¾ inch

TECHNIQUES

Chapter 2

- "Pulling and Cutting Beading Thread"
- "Threading a Beading Needle"
- "Positioning the Needle"
- "Using a Stop Bead"

- "Picking Up Beads"
- "Using a Thread Burner"
- "How to Read a Bead Key"
- "Common Beadwork Terms"

TOOLS AND MATERIALS

- 6-pound FireLine beading thread in crystal
- Ruler (for measuring thread)
- Size 10 beading needle
- 2 pronged, 13mm flat-pad, silver-plated clip-on earring backs*
- 2 perforated 12mm silver-plated disc findings*
- 2 Lucite 12mm aspen leaves in frost green (**A**)*
- 2 green size 11/0 round seed beads; the example uses matte transparent green (**B**)

- 24 Lucite baby's breath flowers in your choice of color; the example uses frost crystal (**C**)*
- 30 size 11/0 seed beads in your choice of color; the example uses silver-lined rainbow rosaline (**D**)
- 2 size 11/0 seed beads (the example uses green)
- 6 Lucite baby's breath flowers; the example uses frost pink (**E**)*
- 4 size 11/0 round seed beads (for anchoring thread on the backs of the discs)

195

Hydrangea Clip-Ons *(continued)*

TOOLS AND MATERIALS *(continued)*

- Chain nose pliers
- Heavy side cutters (for up to 14-gauge wire)
- Instant bond glue

- E6000 glue with a precision applicator tip

*Look for findings at www.firemountaingems.com and Lucite at www.bellomodo.com.

Make the Hydrangea Clip-Ons

1 Pull and cut 3 feet of FireLine with side cutters.

2 Thread the needle and string on a random-colored size 11/0 seed bead.

3 Position the bead about 4 inches from the loose end of the thread and tie a square knot over the bead to secure it (see the FAQ "How do I make a square knot in beading thread?" in Chapter 2).

4 Pass up through the perforated disc hole that is labeled a in the diagrams below.

5 Pick up 1A and 1B, and slide them all the way down.

6 Pass the needle back down through the 1A and the same hole in the disc.

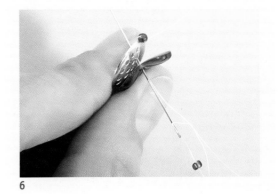

6

View from convex side of disc:

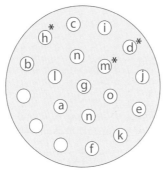

View from concave side of disc:

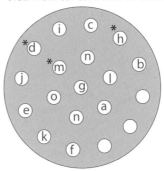

*Use the second color of baby's breath (E) for these.

7 Pull the thread taut to tighten down the leaf and the seed bead against the front of the disc.

8 Pass up through the disc hole labeled b in the diagrams on the previous page.

9 Pick up 1C and 1D, slide them down, and pass down through the 1C and the same hole in the disc.

10 Pull the thread taut again to tighten these beads against the front of the disc.

7

10

11 Continue this process to stitch a flower and a seed bead through each of the disc holes indicated in the diagrams, in alphabetical order. Stitch Cs for c, e, f, g, i, j, k, l, and n; and stitch Es for d, h, and m. Notice that when you get to h, the flowers begin to stack on top of the flowers you stitched in the previous round. Be sure to pass your needle up between existing flowers, and not up through those flowers' holes.

12 Pass up through the hole labeled a, the leaf, and the seed bead that you initially stitched on top of the leaf.

13 Pick up 1C and 1D, and pass down through the 1C, the initial seed bead and leaf, and the same hole in the disc.

14 Pull the thread taut again.

15 Pick up a random-colored size 11/0 bead.

16 Pull both ends of the thread taut at the same time, and tie them in a square knot.

17 Apply a tiny drop of instant bond glue to the knot.

18 Trim the thread ends close to the knot.

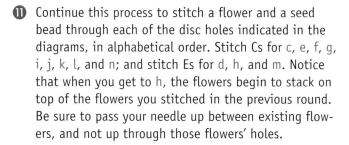

12

13

18

⑲ Pick up one of the clip-on earring backs.

⑳ Use chain nose pliers to slightly bend each prong toward the center of the flat pad.

㉑ Place the beaded disc between the prongs on the flat pad. (If the prongs are bent too far to accommodate the disc, use the pliers to bend them back slightly and then try again.)

㉒ Turn the disc as needed until the leaf is in the position you want it to have when you wear your earrings. In the example, the tip of the leaf points toward the back of the ear.

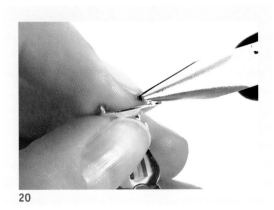

20

㉓ Use chain nose pliers to firmly squeeze down each prong against the disc. You may need to gently nudge the flowers away to make space for your pliers.

㉔ Apply a daub of E6000 to the back of the leaf, between the leaf and the surface of the disc.

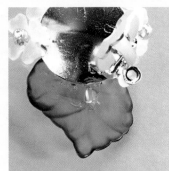

㉕ Repeat steps 1–24 to make a second, matching earring. For Step 22, position the leaf so that it points in the opposite direction as the leaf in your first earring.

㉖ Allow the E6000 to dry for at least 24 hours before wearing your new earrings.

Just like with the Beaded Pinwheel Clip-Ons, you can make the Hydrangea Clip-Ons in different colors. The second example on the right uses baby's breath in violet and yellow, along with beige-lined crystal seed beads.

Moxy Clusters

Learn some bead embroidery techniques while making these chunky, beaded cluster earrings.

Estimated time to complete: 2 hours (plus 24 hours for the glue to cure)   ●   **Approximate diameter:** ⅞ inch

TECHNIQUES
Chapter 2

- "Pulling and Cutting Beading Thread"
- "Pre-stretching Nylon Thread"
- "Waxing or Conditioning Nylon Thread"
- "Threading a Beading Needle"

- "Positioning the Needle"
- "Picking Up Beads"
- "Making Half Hitch Knots"
- "How to Read a Bead Key"

TOOLS AND MATERIALS

- Fabric scissors
- Beading scissors
- Scissors for paper
- Utility shears (heavy household scissors)
- Nicole's Bead Backing in a color that matches or coordinates with your beads*
- Ultrasuede fabric in a color that matches or coordinates with your beads*
- Sheet of tracing paper, or printer paper if you download the template at www.wiley.com/go/earringsvisualprojectguide
- Fine-tip permanent marker
- Size D nylon beading thread in a color that matches or coordinates with your beads
- Thread conditioner (for preparing thread)
- Size 10 beading needle
- 6 Czech fire-polished 8mm glass beads in the color of your choice; the example uses Picasso green turquoise (**A**)*

- 2 glass, 3mm cube beads in any color (**B**)
- About 200 size 11/0 round Japanese seed beads in your choice of color; the example uses silver-lined light gold (**C**)
- Lid from a disposable plastic food container (thin enough to cut with utility shears)
- E6000 glue and white glue
- Pair of 6mm round pad earring posts (the example uses gold-plated posts)
- Pair of matching 12mm comfort back earring post backs
- Hobby knife (such as an Xacto)

*Look for Nicole's Bead Backing, ultrasuede, and interesting colors and finishes of fire-polished beads at www.etsy.com.

Make the Moxy Clusters

① Use fabric scissors to cut two 1-inch squares of backing. (You can use the first square as a cutting template for the second.)

② Trace the circle template at right onto paper (or print it at www.wiley.com/go/earringsvisualprojectguide), and use scissors to cut it out.

③ Center the circle on one of the squares of backing and use a fine-tip permanent marker to trace around it. Repeat on the second square. Set the paper circle template aside to use again later.

④ Prepare about 2½ feet of beading thread, and thread the needle.

⑤ Tie 2 overhand knots, one on top of the other, about 6 inches from the loose end of the thread.

NOTE: To make an overhand knot, loop the thread over itself, pass the end of the thread through the loop, and pull to cinch the knot down.

3

⑥ Pass the needle up from beneath one of the squares of backing, sewing through the circle outline on the front.

⑦ Pull the thread all the way through until the knot rests against the back of the backing.

⑧ Pick up 1A, and slide it down against the front of the backing.

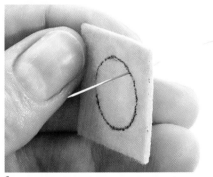

6

9 Nudge this bead back a little so that its end slightly covers the spot where the thread comes through the backing.

10 Sew down through the backing, on the circle outline, at the other end of the bead. Push the needle down at an approximate 45-degree angle so that the thread is hidden beneath the bead.

11 Pull the thread gently taut.

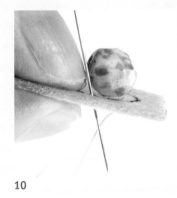

10

11

12 Sew back up through the backing on the circle outline a few millimeters from where you stitched down.

13 String another 1A, and slide it down against the backing.

14 Nudge the 1A back so that it touches (or nearly touches) the previous bead, and then stitch back down through backing, on the circle outline, at a 45-degree angle beneath the end of the bead.

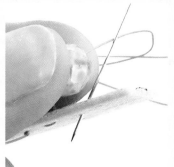
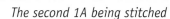

14

The second 1A being stitched

The completed stitch

15 Continue this process to stitch a total of 5 beads onto the circle outline. Try to keep the beads flat so that their holes are parallel to the backing. (If you have lots of empty space on your outline after stitching 5 beads, your beads may not lie flat; pull out the stitches and try again.)

16 Sew up through the circle outline in front of the next bead in the circle, and then pass through the holes of all 5 beads again.

16

⓱ Pass through the first bead again, and then back down through the backing on the circle outline. Pull the thread taut.

⓲ Sew up through the backing near the center of the circle, and string 1B.

⓳ Slide the 1B down against the backing, and then sew down through the backing again. (This bead does not need to be perfectly centered; it is not visible in the completed design.)

19

⓴ Sew up through the backing just past one end of the 1B, and string 1A.

㉑ Sew down through the backing just past the other end of the 1B, and pull the thread taut.

㉒ Sew up through the circle outline halfway between any 2 beads, keeping the needle outside the thread that runs between those beads.

21

22

㉓ Pick up 13C, and sew back down through the backing halfway between the next 2 beads in the circle, but up against the center 1A (rather than through the circle outline).

㉔ Pull the thread taut.

24

25. Sew up through the circle outline halfway between the next 2 beads in the circle.

26. Repeat steps 23–24 to stitch another set of 13C.

27. Continue this process all the way around the circle, for a total of 5 sets of 13C.

28. Turn the beadwork over and remove the needle.

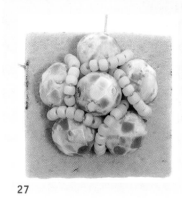

27

30

29. Tie a square knot against the back side of the backing with the 2 thread tails.

30. Trim the tails to about ¼ inch from the knot.

31. Use fabric scissors to make 5 straight cuts through the backing around the circle of beads, creating a hexagon. Cut close to the beads, but leave a small (about 2mm) border of backing for stitching a round of seed beads later. Be careful not to cut through any stitches.

31

32

32. Trim off the tips of each corner, continuing to leave a small space for stitching seed beads later.

33. Use the paper circle template and the marker to trace a circle onto the lid of a disposable plastic food container (a deli takeout container is used in the example).

34. Use utility shears to cut out the circle. Cut directly on the line; it's better that the plastic circle be too small than too large.

34

35 Apply a dab of E6000 to the pad on one of the earring posts, and press it down onto the plastic circle. Position the post close to one edge of the circle; if it is farther down, the weight of the earrings may make them fall too far forward when you wear them.

36 Hold the post against the plastic for 20 seconds, and then set it aside for 12–24 hours to cure.

36

37 Cut out a second plastic circle, and glue on the other earring back (for the second earring) so that they cure at the same time.

38 While the E6000 is drying, repeat steps 4–32 for the second earring.

39 When the E6000 has cured, coat the back of each plastic circle (the side without an earring post) with white glue.

40 Adhere the plastic circles to the backs of the earrings, with the posts aligned at the top center of each earring; however, be sure to leave a small border (about 2mm) of backing between the plastic circle and the edge of the backing. This is where you will stitch on the final seed beads later.

40

41 Use fabric scissors to cut out two 1¼-inch squares of ultrasuede.

42 Use a hobby knife to make a small cut in each square for each earring post to pass through. Make these cuts far enough away from the edges that the ultrasuede will completely cover the back of each earring.

42

43 Apply a drop of white glue to the plastic circle on each earring.

44 Slide each ultrasuede square over each post, and press the ultrasuede down against the back of the earring. If your ultrasuede has a "right" side and a "wrong" side, make sure the right side is facing outward.

45 Use fabric scissors to cut the ultrasuede to match the size and shape of the bead backing.

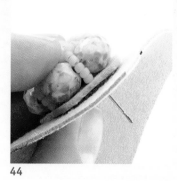

44   45

46 Prepare another 2½-foot length of beading thread, and thread the needle.

47 Tie a double overhand knot an inch or two from the loose end.

48 Working one of the earrings, sew up through the bead backing 1mm in from the edge, but do not pass through the ultrasuede; nudge the ultrasuede aside, as shown.

48

49 Pull the thread taut, and then tuck the short thread tail at least partially beneath the ultrasuede. (If the end hangs out on the other side, you can trim it off later.)

50 Pick up 1C, and sew back down through both the backing and the ultrasuede.

51 Pull the thread taut again, and then bring the needle up around the edge of the backing and ultrasuede, and pass it behind the thread exiting the 1C that you just stitched.

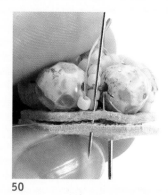

50   51

52 Pull the thread gently taut, and pick up another 1C.

53 Sew back down through the backing and the ultra-suede on the other side of the 1C, and pull the thread taut again.

54 Bring the needle around the edges of the backing and ultrasuede and behind the thread that exits the last 1C. Pull the thread taut again.

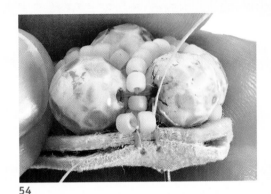

54

55 Repeat this process to stitch 1C at a time all the way around the edge of the earring. Keep the stitches as neat and uniform as you can.

56 When you finish, pass the needle through all the edge beads at least once for reinforcement. Pull the thread taut and tie a few half hitch knots along the way.

57 Bring the needle out, and cut the thread close to the beadwork.

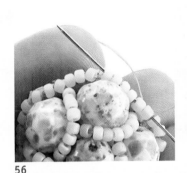

56

57

58 Trim off the short thread tail from when you began stitching the edge beads (unless it is fully hidden beneath the ultrasuede).

59 Repeat steps 46–58 to stitch edge beads around the second earring, and weave-in and trim off the thread.

60 Secure the post backs to your earrings to complete the pair.

You can make these showy earrings in lots of different color combinations. Naturally, your bead-embroidered earrings are not water resistant, so take care to keep them clean and dry.

60

CHAPTER 9

Sparkle and Glam

The earrings in this chapter are designed to dazzle with cubic zirconia, rhinestones, and crystals.

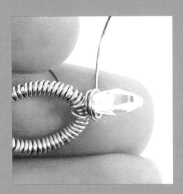

Empire Crystal Ball Earrings

The Czech crystal settings in these earrings reflect light in all directions and provide subtle vintage flair.

Specifications

Estimated time to complete: 25 minutes • **Approximate length:** 1¼ inches

TECHNIQUES
Chapter 2

- "Open and Close Simple Connector Loops"
- "Pulling and Cutting Beading Thread"
- "Threading a Beading Needle"
- "Positioning the Needle"

- "Using a Stop Bead"
- "Picking Up Beads"
- "Using a Thread Burner"
- "How to Read a Bead Key"
- "Common Beadwork Terms"

TOOLS AND MATERIALS

- 6-pound FireLine beading thread in crystal
- Hobby knife, children's craft scissors, or side cutters (for cutting FireLine thread)
- 24 size 15/0 round Miyuki seed beads in color-lined white rainbow (**A**)
- 20 size 11/0 round Miyuki seed beads in color-lined crystal rainbow (**B**)
- 8 Preciosa 8mm silver-tone, AB crystal ball beads (**C**)*

- 2 Preciosa 2mm x 5mm Czech Twin beads in clear crystal (**D**)*
- Size 10 English beading needle
- Size 11/0 round seed bead (stop bead)
- Thread burner
- Pair of ready-made, 4mm ball-end, silver-plate earring posts with connector loops
- Matching earring backs

*Look for these at store.goodybeads.com.

Make the Empire Crystal Ball Earrings

1 Pull and cut 3 feet of FireLine, thread the needle, and attach a stop bead about 8 inches from the loose end of the thread. (Use a hobby knife, children's craft scissors, or side cutters to cut the FireLine.)

2 String 3A, 1B, 1C, 1B, 1D, 2B, 1C, 1A, 1B, 1A, 1C, 1A, 1B, 1A, 1C, 1A, 1B, and 1A, and slide them down against the stop bead.

3 Pass through the second C that you strung (in the same direction), and pull the thread gently taut.

4 Pass (again) through the next 1A, 1B, 1A, 1C, 1A, 1B, 1A, and 1C (all of which you strung in Step 2).

5 Hold the beads between your fingers, and pull the thread gently taut again.

6 Pick up 2B, and pass up through the empty hole in the 1D.

7 Pick up 1B, pass back through the first C and B that you strung, and pull the thread taut.

8 Pick up 3A and one of the earring posts, and slide them down against the B.

9 Remove the stop bead by sliding it off the thread, and then make a square knot with both ends of the thread (see the FAQ "How do I make a square knot in beading thread?" in Chapter 2).

2

3

4

7

9

10 Pass down through the 3A and 1B and through the next 1C, 1B, 1D, 2B, 1C, 1A, and 1B in the beadwork.

11 Pull the thread taut, and trim it close to the beadwork with a thread burner.

12 Thread the needle on the remaining thread tail.

13 Pass down through the other side of the beadwork, and bring the needle out through the B that is just across from the last 1B in Step 10.

14 Pull the thread taut, and trim it close to the beadwork with the thread burner.

13

15 Slide an earring back onto the earring post to complete the first earring.

16 Repeat steps 1–15 to complete a second, matching earring (a).

As a variation on this design, you can use black, instead of clear, Twin beads (b).

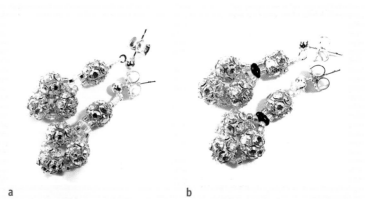

a

b

Bejeweled Chain Earrings

Varying lengths of sparkling rhinestone chain hang from ready-made earring posts for an elegant, romantic effect.

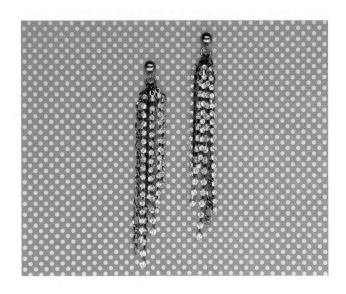

Specifications

Estimated time to complete: 25 minutes ● **Approximate length:** 3¾ inches

TECHNIQUES
Chapter 2

- "Open and Close Jump Rings"
- "Cut Closed-Link Chain"

TOOLS AND MATERIALS
Look for all these items at www.rings-things.com.

- 14½ inches of 3mm clear crystal rhinestone chain in gunmetal
- 14½ inches of 2mm clear crystal rhinestone chain in gunmetal
- 6 ring-end 3mm rhinestone chain ends in gunmetal
- 6 ring-end 2mm rhinestone chain ends in gunmetal
- 6½ inches of 7mm figaro chain in gunmetal (or your choice of gunmetal chain)

- 6 oval 3mm x 4mm 20-gauge jump rings in gunmetal
- 2 round 5mm 18-gauge jump rings in gunmetal
- 2 ready-made earring posts in gunmetal with 6mm balls and connector rings
- 2 "comfort"-style earring backs in silver tone or gunmetal
- Side cutters
- 2 pairs of chain nose pliers
- Ruler (for measuring chain)

Bejeweled Chain Earrings *(continued)*

Make the Bejeweled Chain Earrings

1. Use side cutters to cut a segment of 3mm rhinestone chain that is 9 rhinestone settings long. Cut the metal tab that connects the settings close to the last setting in your segment, and remove as much of the tab as you can.

2. Place a setting at the end of the segment between the prongs on one of the 3mm rhinestone chain ends. Press the setting all the way down.

3. Holding a pair of chain nose pliers at a 45-degree angle to the chain end, gently squeeze down the chain end to bend one of the prongs until it rests on the surface of the rhinestone.

4. Use the same technique to press down the prong on the other side of the chain end.

5. Use side cutters to cut a segment of 2mm rhinestone chain that is 14 settings long.

6. Use chain nose pliers to attach a 2mm chain end to that segment of chain.

7. Use 2 pairs of chain nose pliers to open one of the oval jump rings.

8. Slide the connector ring on the 3mm chain end from Step 2 onto the jump ring.

6

8

214

⑨ Slide the ring on the 2mm chain end from Step 6 onto the jump ring on top of the 3mm chain. Make sure that both chains face the same direction.

⑩ Use 2 pairs of chain nose pliers to close the jump ring.

⑪ Cut a new segment of 3mm rhinestone chain that is 13 settings long, and attach a 3mm chain end.

⑫ Cut a new segment of 2mm chain that is 12 settings long, and attach a 2mm chain end.

9

⑬ Slide the 3mm chain segment onto an open oval jump ring.

⑭ Slide the 2mm chain segment onto the jump ring, facing the same direction as the 3mm chain.

⑮ Close the jump ring.

⑯ Cut a new segment of 3mm rhinestone chain that is 16 settings long, attach a 3mm chain end, and slide it onto an open oval jump ring.

Steps 1–15 completed

⑰ Cut a segment of 2mm rhinestone chain that is 17 settings long, attach a 2mm chain end, and slide it onto the jump ring facing the same direction.

⑱ Check the ends of all 6 segments of chain for protruding metal tabs that you cut to separate the chain (see photo). Use side cutters to cut them off.

⑲ Use side cutters to cut a length of gunmetal chain that is just over 3 inches long. (If you use chain with open links, you can open one of the links with chain nose pliers instead.)

⑳ Use 2 pairs of chain nose pliers to open one of the round, 18-gauge jump rings.

㉑ Slide on the segment of gunmetal chain.

19

㉒ Attach the oval jump ring on the third pair of rhinestone chain segments that you made (from steps 16–17) to the round jump ring.

㉓ Attach the second pair of rhinestone chain segments (with the chains from steps 11–12) to the round jump ring, making sure that they face the same direction as the segments you attached in Step 22.

㉔ Attach the remaining pair of rhinestone chain segments to the round jump ring, making sure that they face the same direction as the first 2 pairs.

㉕ Slide one of the ear posts onto the round jump ring, making sure that its ball end faces the same direction as the rhinestone chains.

26 Use 2 pairs of chain nose pliers to close the round jump ring.

27 Perform steps 1–26 to create a second, matching earring, but arrange the chains in the *opposite* order on the round jump ring. This ensures that the earrings are mirror images of one another when you wear them.

26

28 Attach the earring backs to complete your pair.

To make a quick pair of formal earrings in a hurry, try cutting two single settings (or two multi-setting segments) from a rhinestone chain and gluing them to gluable pad earring posts.

1. Select ready-made earring posts with pads that are smaller than your rhinestones.

2. Clean each pad and the back of each setting with a cotton swab dipped in rubbing alcohol.

3. Use a toothpick to apply a small amount of clear, two-part epoxy glue, or E6000, to the center of each gluable pad.

4. Press each setting onto each pad, and hold it there for several seconds.

5. Allow the glue to set for the time recommended on the package.

The earrings in the example use 6mm rhinestone chain and 4mm pad ear posts.

Medallion Crystal Fringe Earrings

M ake these dramatic earrings by
layering gold filigree and adding a
fringe of crystal bicones on head pins.

Specifications

Estimated time to complete: 45 minutes ● **Approximate length:** 3¼ inches

TECHNIQUES

Chapter 2

- "Straighten, Cut, and File Wire"

- "Bend, Shape, and Hammer Wire"

- "Make and Use Simple Connector Loops and Jump Rings"

- "How to Read a Bead Key"

Chapter 3

- "Bail-Maker French Hooks"

TOOLS AND MATERIALS

- 2 laser-cut 40mm round filigree drops in raw brass (look for these at www.rings-things.com)

- 2 gold-plated 37mm round iron filigree stamp-ings (look for these on www.etsy.com)

- 12 inches of 28-gauge, round, tarnish-resistant gold-finish craft wire (such as Bead Smith wire)

- 22 brass (or gold-plated) 20-gauge, 1½- or 2-inch head pins

- About 4 inches of 20-gauge brass wire

- Ruler (for measuring wire)

- 66 Chinese crystal 3mm bicone beads in topaz (**A**)

- 32 Chinese crystal 4mm bicone beads in tanzanite luster (**B**)

- 34 Chinese crystal 4mm bicone beads in black diamond luster (**C**)

- Side cutters

- Flat nose, chain nose, and round nose pliers

- Bail-making pliers; flat nylon jaw pliers; chasing hammer; steel bench block; and medium-cut, flat needle file (for making ear wires)

- 2 brass or gold-plated 20-gauge, 4.5mm outside-diameter jump rings

Make the Medallion Crystal Fringe Earrings

1 Use your fingers to gently straighten a little over 6 inches of 28-gauge wire still on the spool.

2 Cut a 6-inch length of the wire.

3 Bend the wire in half to form a long "U" shape.

4 Center the stamping on top of the filigree, and thread one end of the wire through the center top piercings in the stamping and the filigree, front to back.

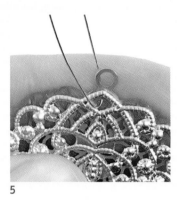
5

6

5 Pull the wire through until the bottom of the "U" rests against the stamping.

6 While using your finger to hold the wire against the stamping, gently wrap one end of the wire around the edge of the stamping and filigree, as shown.

7 Using either end of the wire, make a second wrap beside the first.

7

8

8 Pass the wire through the piercing to bring it over to the other side of the connector loop on the filigree.

9 Use the same process to make 2 matching wraps there.

10 Bring both wire ends to the back of the filigree, use side cutters to trim both wires close to the wraps (a), and use the tips of chain nose pliers to press them flat (b).

10a

10b

⑪ Straighten and cut a second 6-inch length of wire, and use the same process to make 2 matching sets of double wraps at the bottom centers of the stamping and the filigree. Because the stamping does not reach the bottom of the filigree, you need to make these wraps inside the stamping and filigree rather than at the edge. This method is called *stitching* with wire.

⑫ String the following beads on a head pin: 1B, 1A, 1C, 1A, 1B, 1A.

11

⑬ Use side cutters to flush-cut the pin to about ³⁄₈ inch past the last A.

⑭ Grasp the head pin with flat nose pliers just past the last A.

⑮ Use the pliers to bend the head pin 90 degrees.

⑯ Use round nose pliers to roll the end of the head pin into a loop.

15

16

⑰ Use flat nose pliers to open the loop, and then slide it through the bottom center piercing in the filigree.

⑱ Use the flat nose pliers to close the loop.

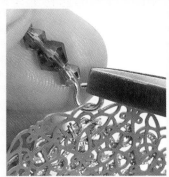

19 String the following beads on another head pin: 1C, 1A, 1B, 1A, 1C, 1A.

20 Repeat steps 13–16 to create a loop.

21 Using flat nose pliers to open and close the loop, attach this head pin to a piercing in the filigree adjacent to the first head pin.

22 Make 4 more beaded head pins, alternating between the pattern of beads used in Step 12 and in Step 19 for each pin.

21

23 Equally space and attach those pins to the filigree stamping, working your way upward on the stamping.

24 Make 5 more beaded head pins, beginning with the pattern from Step 19 and alternating between the 2 patterns with each additional pin.

25 Attach those pins to the other half of the filigree, mirroring the placement of the pins on the first half.

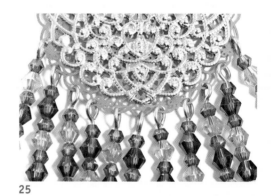

25

26 Repeat steps 1–25 to make a second fringed medallion.

27 Use 20-gauge wire to make a pair of Bail-Maker French Hooks.

28 Use the jump rings to attach the top loops on the medallions to the bottom loops on the ear wires.

Gypsy Princess Drops

Express your playful side with these whimsical drop earrings that feature Swarovski rhinestones set in Apoxie clay.

Specifications

Estimated time to complete: 45 minutes, plus 48 hours to cure ● **Approximate length:** 1¾ inches

TECHNIQUES
Chapter 2

- "Open and Close Simple Connector Loops"

- "Open and Close Jump Rings"
- "Cut Closed-Link Chain"

TOOLS AND MATERIALS

- 2 nickel-free, silver-plated brass 30mm x 16mm teardrops (item #H20-1393FX)*

- About 4 inches of 4mm Swarovski gold-plated rhinestone chain in crystal (look for this at www.rings-things.com)

- 2 JBB findings 10mm gold-plated pewter round connector rings (look for these at www.beadaholique.com)

- About 36 crystal rhinestone 1mm chatons*

TOOLS AND MATERIALS (CONTINUED)

- Side cutters
- Apoxie Sculpt two-part modeling clay in black*
- 1 or 2 pairs of disposable latex or nitrile gloves
- Paper towels
- ¼ teaspoon measuring spoon (reserved for craft use)
- Toothpicks
- Hobby knife
- Beeswax
- E6000 glue
- Cardboard as a work surface
- Pearl Ex pigment color in pink flamingo (look for this at a craft store)
- Dust mask

- Wooden craft sticks
- Disposable plastic container
- Toothbrush or soft vegetable brush (reserved for craft use)
- Rubbing alcohol and cotton swabs
- Flat nose and chain nose pliers
- 2 silver-plated 4mm ball-end stud ear posts with connector rings and matching "comfort"-style earring backs
- 4 silver-plate 4mm round 20-gauge jump rings
- Mild dish or hand soap and hand towel
- Optional but recommended: Magnifier

*Look for these items at www.firemountaingems.com.

Make the Gypsy Princess Drops

1 Use side cutters to cut 2 single rhinestones off the rhinestone chain. Cut directly through the flat metal connector between settings and remove as much of the connector as you can.

2 Cut 2 segments of chain that are 8 rhinestones long each, and set them aside.

3 Put on disposable gloves, and open both pots of Apoxie Sculpt.

4 Use the measuring spoon to scoop out ¼ teaspoon of the gray component. Level it off with your fingers.

5 Remove the ball of gray material from the spoon (scraping it with a wooden craft stick, if necessary), and place the material on your cardboard work surface.

6 Use a paper towel to wipe out the measuring spoon until it looks clean.

4

7 Scoop out ¼ teaspoon of the black component. Do your best to make it exactly equal to the amount of gray component you scooped. (The closer the proportions are to 50:50, the more successfully the Apoxie Sculpt sets.)

8 Remove the black component from the spoon and set it aside, and then wipe the spoon clean with a paper towel.

9 Securely close both pots of Apoxie Sculpt.

7

⓾ Knead the ¼ teaspoon of black component and the ¼ teaspoon of gray component between your fingers for a full 2 minutes (a). Fold and press the 2 parts together so that the gray material becomes fully incorporated into the black (b).

a

b

⓫ After removing your gloves, tear off a small ball of the mixed Apoxie Sculpt, and press it into the bezel cup on one of the teardrops.

⓬ Use your fingers to shape the Apoxie Sculpt into an even, relatively flat layer within the bezel cup. Remove and discard any excess material that comes up over the sides.

⓭ Repeat Step 12 with the second teardrop.

11

⓮ Use a paper towel to wipe the sides and edges of the teardrop, removing any excess Apoxie Sculpt.

⓯ Use your fingers to gently press a gold-plated connector ring into the Apoxie Sculpt in the lower part of each teardrop. Make the top surface of each ring almost, but not quite, flush with the surface of the Apoxie Sculpt.

12

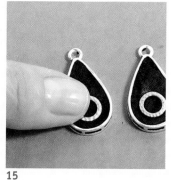

15

16. Press each single rhinestone setting into the Apoxie Sculpt above each gold ring, leaving a small space between the rhinestone and the gold ring, as shown.

17. Use a hobby knife to cut a piece of beeswax that is just larger than the tip of a toothpick.

18. Roll the piece of beeswax between your fingers to warm it and form it into a ball.

19. Press the ball of beeswax onto the end of a toothpick.

20. Pour out a small pile of crystal chatons.

21. Use the waxed end of the toothpick to pick up 1 chaton, touching the top of the chaton with the wax.

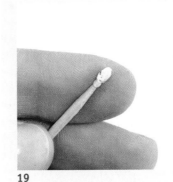

19

23

22. Gently place the chaton down into the Apoxie Sculpt inside one of the embedded connector rings so that the entire pointed bottom of the chaton is covered with Apoxie Sculpt.

23. Add more chatons inside the ring until no more will fit without misplacing the others. (You may find it easier to place the stones if you use a magnifier.)

24. Add a single chaton below the ring, 1 above the gold ring, and 2 more above the rhinestone setting, as shown. (Optionally, you can create a different design or use more or fewer chatons.)

24

25 Wipe the sides of the teardrop with a paper towel to remove any Apoxie Sculpt that has seeped out.

26 Use the wax-tipped toothpick to place a single chaton in each of the top 3 slots on each side of the teardrop.

27 Repeat steps 21–26 to adorn the other teardrop with chatons.

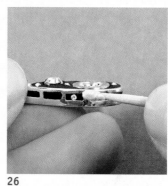

25
26

28 Place both teardrops in a disposable plastic tray or container.

29 Put on a dust mask, and use a craft stick to pour artist pigment over the top of each teardrop.

30 Set the container aside for 24 hours to allow the Apoxie Sculpt to fully cure.

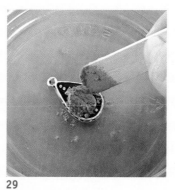
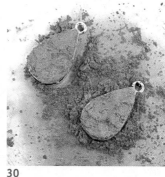

29
30

31 With your dust mask on, pick up each teardrop and tap off the pigment on the inside of the plastic container. (The pigment is messy, so you may want to put on another pair of rubber gloves for this step.)

32 Brush each teardrop with a toothbrush or soft vegetable brush in a circular motion to remove most of the excess pigment. (You can pour the pigment back into the pigment jar for reuse.)

33 Wash each teardrop in mild hand or dish soap, blot it dry with a towel, and allow it to air-dry completely.

32

34 Use a cotton swab dipped in rubbing alcohol to clean the edges of the rhinestone settings along one side of each chain segment that you cut in Step 2.

35 Working in a well-ventilated area, squeeze a small amount of E6000 onto a piece of cardboard.

36 Use a toothpick or small craft stick to apply a generous amount of E6000 to one side of each rhinestone setting for the entire length of each chain.

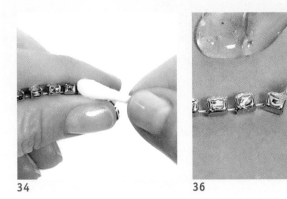

34

36

37 One at a time, press each chain onto each teardrop. Center the chain so that its first and last rhinestone settings are aligned evenly horizontally, and hold it securely against the teardrop with your fingers for at least 30 seconds.

38 Set the teardrops aside, and allow the E6000 to cure for 24 hours.

37

39 When the glue has cured, use flat nose and chain nose pliers to link 2 jump rings, and use them to attach the top ring on each teardrop to the connector ring on each ear post.

Zirconia Array Earrings

In this design, sparkling synthetic gemstone cubic zirconia contrasts elegantly with the more casual wire wraps embracing them.

Specifications

Estimated time to complete: 1 hour ● **Approximate length:** 1³⁄₄ inches

TECHNIQUES

Chapter 2

- "Straighten, Cut, and File Wire"

- "Bend, Shape, and Hammer Wire"

- "Open and Close Jump Rings"

- "Wrap Wire Over Wire"

- "Create a Patina with Liver of Sulfur"

Chapter 3

- "Circular French Hooks"

TOOLS AND MATERIALS

- 4 inches of 18-gauge, dead-soft, round sterling silver or silver-filled wire

- 40 inches of 24-gauge, dead-soft, round bronze wire

- 32 inches of 26-gauge, dead-soft, round bronze wire

- About 4 inches of 20-gauge, dead-soft, round sterling silver or silver-filled wire

- 2 sterling silver or silver-filled, 5mm outside diameter, 18-gauge jump rings

- 4 cubic zirconia 6mm x 6mm flat briolette tear-drops in clear

- 2 cubic zirconia 5mm x 7mm flat briolette tear-drops in clear

- Flat nylon jaw pliers

- Ruler (for measuring wire)

- Side cutters

- Medium-cut, flat needle file

- 12mm mandrel (a retractable permanent marker was used for the example)

- Round nose pliers

- Steel bench block and chasing hammer

- 2 pairs of chain nose pliers

- Liver of sulfur, fine steel wool, and additional patina supplies

229

Make the Zirconia Array Earrings

① Use flat nylon jaw pliers to straighten several inches of 18-gauge silver wire still on the spool.

② Flush-cut two 2-inch lengths of the 18-gauge wire and flat-file their ends.

③ Use round nose pliers to make small loops at the ends of each wire, with both loops facing the same direction. Make these loops large enough to accommodate 5mm jump rings (which you attach later).

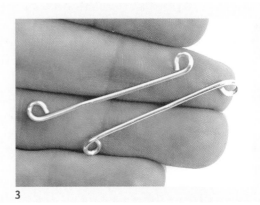

3

④ Bend one of the wires around a 12mm mandrel, with the loops facing away from the mandrel.

NOTE: If the loops on the wire become bent, use flat nylon jaw pliers to straighten them.

⑤ Use a steel bench block and chasing hammer to lightly flatten the large curve in the wire.

⑥ Use your fingers to squeeze the 2 small loops slightly toward one another.

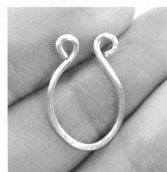

7 Use your fingers to gently straighten 20 inches of 24-gauge bronze wire still on the spool.

8 Use side cutters to trim that 20 inches off the spool.

9 Use flat nose pliers to bend the last inch of the 24-gauge wire into a narrow "U," and then slide it over the curved 18-gauge wire near one of the small loops.

10 Press the short wire tail against the loop on the 18-gauge wire for leverage, and start making tightly stacked wraps. Use the tip of your index finger to position each new wrap against the previous wrap.

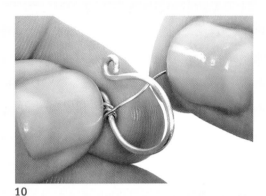

10

11 Keep wrapping until the unlooped portion of 18-gauge wire is covered with wraps. You may find it helpful to stop occasionally and use chain nose pliers to neaten the wraps.

12 Trim both wire ends, and press them down with the tips of chain nose pliers.

13 Use your fingers to press the looped ends of the 18-gauge wire toward one another so that they overlap.

12

13

The wraps completed

14 Attach a jump ring to the stacked loops. (If the loops are still too far apart, squeeze them together with nylon jaw pliers.)

15 Gently straighten and cut 16 inches of 26-gauge bronze wire.

16 Bend the wire in half (into a long "U" shape).

17 Slide the "U" over the bottom center of the loop of wrapped 18-gauge wire from the inside.

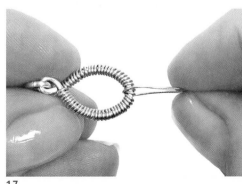

17

⑱ String one 5mm x 7mm cubic zirconia bead onto one end of the 26-gauge wire, and slide the bead down to the wrapped 18-gauge wire.

⑲ Cross the 2 ends of the 26-gauge wire and position the teardrop so that its tip points toward the bottom curve of the 18-gauge wire, as shown.

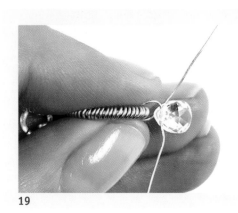

19

⑳ Push one end of the 26-gauge wire through the center of the wrapped 18-gauge loop (a), and wrap it around the 18-gauge wire one time (b). Leave a small space between the tip of the teardrop and the wraps on the 18-gauge wire (otherwise, the tip of the teardrop may break). You may need to use your fingers to hold the teardrop in place as you make the wrap.

a

b

㉑ Slowly wrap the same end of the 26-gauge wire around the top of the bead 4 complete times.

㉒ Wrap the 26-gauge wire around the wrapped 18-gauge wire once on the opposite side of the teardrop on which you made wraps in Step 20.

㉓ String a 6mm x 6mm cubic zirconia bead onto the same end of the 26-gauge wire.

㉔ Wrap it onto the 18-gauge wire the same way you wrapped the first teardrop.

㉕ Make 2 or 3 more wraps with the 26-gauge wire, trim it close to the wraps, and use the tips of chain nose pliers to press it down.

24

25

㉖ Pass the other end of the 26-gauge wire through the center of the wrapped loop of 18-gauge wire, and then wrap it around the 18-gauge wire one complete time.

㉗ String on a 6mm x 6mm bead, and wrap it the same way you wrapped the first 2 beads.

㉘ Make a few more wraps, trim the wire, and press down its end.

㉙ Repeat steps 4–28 to complete a second earring drop.

㉚ Use 20-gauge wire to make a pair of Circular French Hooks, and attach them to the jump rings on the drops.

㉛ Use liver of sulfur to darken the metal on each earring, and lightly brush back the color using fine steel wool.

Most of the jewelry making tools and supplies used in this book are available online from the suppliers listed here.

GENERAL SUPPLIES

These suppliers stock jewelry making essentials, including beading and wirework supplies. Some also carry more specialized tools and materials.

- Artbeads.com (www.artbeads.com)
- BelloModo (www.bellomodo.com)
- Fire Mountain Gems & Beads (www.firemountaingems.com)
- Fusion Beads (www.fusionbeads.com)
- JewelrySupply.com (www.jewelrysupply.com)
- Rings & Things (www.rings-things.com; $50 minimum order)

METAL WORK SUPPLIES

These suppliers carry a variety of general metal work tools and materials.

- Contenti (www.contenti.com)
- Otto Frei (www.ottofrei.com)
- Rio Grande (www.riogrande.com)

ADHESIVES AND RESIN

These suppliers carry inventories of craft adhesives and resins and related supplies.

- Blick (www.dickblick.com)
- Lisa Pavelka (www.lisapavelka.com)
- Resin Obsession (www.resinobsession.com)
- Rings & Things (www.rings-things.com)

CHAIN, STONES, SETTINGS, AND STAMPINGS

Although you can find chain, gemstones, and settings at just about any general supply shop, the suppliers below carry especially interesting treasures.

- B'Sue Boutiques (www.bsueboutiques.com)
- Jan's Jewelry Supplies (www.jansjewels.com)
- The Beadin' Path (www.beadinpath.com)

LEATHER SUPPLIES

You can harvest leather from old clothing, belts, and handbags. For new leather, and the tools and supplies you need to work with it, visit these suppliers.

- eLeatherSupply (www.eleathersupply.com)
- JoAnn Fabric and Craft Stores (for fabric shears and snaps; www.joann.com)
- Tafurious (thingumabobs.etsy.com)
- Tandy Leather Factory (www.tandyleatherfactory.com)

SPECIALTY ITEMS

Finally, here are some resources for unusual and hard-to-find jewelry supplies, organized by item.

BOTTLE CAPS
- Just Becuz (justbecuz11.etsy.com)

CLEAR GLASS CABOCHONS AND TILES
- Beadaholique (www.beadaholique.com)
- Sun and Moon (sunandmooncraftkits.etsy.com)

COLLAGE SHEETS
- Resin Obsession (www.resinobsession.com)
- Stampington & Company (www.stampington.com)

ODDITIES
- PULPmiscellania (pulpmiscellania.etsy.com)

POSTAGE STAMPS
- artypharty (artypharty.etsy.com)
- U.S. Postal Service Postal Store (shop.usps.com)

PRINTABLE IMAGES (DOWNLOADS)
- Beadjewelry.net (www.beadjewelry.net/collage_sheets)
- Pixeltwister (pixeltwister.etsy.com)

RIBBON AND LACE
- Beadaholique (www.beadaholique.com)
- the red fairy (theredfairy.etsy.com)

VINTAGE FINDS
- Cool Vintage (coolvintage.etsy.com)

Index